*Running Applied
Psychology Experiments*

Open Guides to Psychology

Series Editor: Judith Greene, Professor of Psychology
at the Open University

Running Applied Psychology Experiments

John Leach

Open University Press
Milton Keynes · Philadelphia

Open University Press
Celtic Court
22 Ballmoor
Buckingham MK18 1XW

and
1990 Frost Road, Suite 101
Bristol, PA 19007, USA

First Published 1991

Copyright © John Leach 1991

British Library Cataloguing-in-Publication Data

Running applied psychology experiments.
– (Open guides to psychology)
  I. Leach, John   II. Series
  158

  ISBN 0–335–09482–1

Library of Congress Cataloging-in-Publication Data

Leach, John, 1953–
    Running applied psychology experiments/John Leach.
      p. cm. — (Open guides to psychology)
    Includes bibliographical references and index.
    ISBN 0–335–09482–1
    1. Psychology, Experimental.   2. Psychology—Experiments.
  3. Experimental design.   I. Title.   II. Series.
  BF181.L42   1991
  150'.724—dc20   91–17918
                                                        CIP

Typeset by Inforum Typesetting, Portsmouth
Printed in Great Britain by St Edmundsbury Press, Bury St Edmunds

Contents

Contents

Preface

This is a practical book. It is deliberately so. The purpose of this guide is to introduce the interested student to that field of psychology which is both rich and complex, both *experimental* and *applied*. This it seeks to do in as painless a manner as possible. It has become all too clear that many able students have been lost to applied experimental psychology because their flame of enthusiasm, fired within academic cloisters, was quickly doused in the soggy reality of the outside world. Yet many of the mistakes made are simple ones which could be easily prevented with a basic appreciation of how things operate *out there*. Moreover, these are the types of mistake which, once made are never repeated. This manual has been written in part to highlight the most common problems which are likely to befall the applied experimentalist and to provide advice on how they can be avoided or overcome. After all, any student who willingly takes an experiment into the outside world demonstrates a degree of courage, and courage in scientific research is our life-blood.

Research takes many forms. It may be a single, one-off experiment, a substantial undergraduate project, a three-year PhD programme or a major 12-year investigation by a multi-national organization. Essentially the principles are the same. As far as this guide is concerned, however, the type of study most commonly referred to is the undergraduate project. There are two reasons for this: firstly, it is the most frequent item of substantive work undertaken by students in behavioural research and secondly, it is the area most fraught with difficulties.

The *project* is the vehicle by which most students sample applied research. Unfortunately, every year projects are submitted which do not meet their full promise because the student has failed to appreciate all the factors involved in setting up, running and decomissioning an applied programme of work. These are the factors which are addressed in this guide.

It is also hoped that this guide will be of benefit to the supervisors and tutors of applied student projects. When a youngster goes to sea for the first time he is put under the care of an old and experienced hand who is known as his 'sea-daddy'. The main role of the sea-daddy is to introduce the recruit to the ways of his newly adopted environment and to 'show him the ropes'. In the academic world the role of sea-daddy should fall to the project supervisor. Unfortunately, it is not as simple as that. It is apparent that many would-be supervisors, although well-versed in their specialist fields, and indeed in the discipline as a whole, do not themselves possess the requisite experience for applied research. Consequently, such supervisors run the risk of committing the same errors as their students.

Preface

Furthermore, it is known for such supervisors to deliberately steer their students away from applied research so that they may be more easily handled within the familiar and convenient (to the tutor, that is) laboratory-based study. If this guide encourages supervisors to take on applied experimental projects then it will have achieved a success.

In producing this guide it has been necessary to assume a basic understanding of scientific design and statistical concepts such as that of 'significance' in the reader. Anyone who does not think that they have a sufficient grasp of these topics is recommended to read two complementary volumes in this series of Open Guides: *Designing and Reporting Experiments* by Peter Harris (1986) and *Learning To Use Statistical Tests in Psychology* by Judith Greene and Manuela D'Oliveira (1990) both published by the Open University Press.

How to use this guide

This guide is designed to be a *pocket manual* to running applied experiments in the field. It is expected that the student will read the main sections initially to obtain an overview of the discipline, and then will concentrate on those sections relevant to his or her phase of research. It is also expected that the guide will be used more as a reference handbook to be dipped into by both student and supervisor rather than as a more conventional textbook. This guide is intended to double as an *aide-mémoire*.

This is an Open Guide and consequently you are expected to be active in acquiring the skills and information contained herein. Unlike many textbooks, however, the aim of this guide is practical application; that is, you do not just read about the topic but go out and do it. Learning will come from both approaches. To support the former this guide is studded with **SAQs – Self-Assessment Questions**. These **SAQs** are designed to give you feedback on your performance. The answers to the **SAQs** are contained at the end of the book. Ultimately, of course, you will have to commit yourself to the field and this is where you will really begin to learn the craft of applied experimental psychology.

Acknowledgements

First and foremost thanks must go to Mrs Sheila Whalley in the Department of Psychology at Lancaster University who carried most of the burden for converting this guide into text. Thanks also go over the years to Prof. Peter Morris, Prof. Philip Levy, Prof. Ray Bull, Dr Duncan Godden and Dr Edward Wilson. The staff, post-graduates and students at the

Department of Psychology, Lancaster University, Jan, Bryony and Freya. All the amenable host organizations and those innumerable real people who volunteered to participate in applied experimental research.

Finally, the author would welcome from readers any comments, suggestions, criticisms, examples or anecdotes which would help to illustrate or to bring this guide further into line with the needs of students and supervisors. He can be reached at the Department of Psychology, University of Lancaster, Lancaster, LA1 4YF.

J.L.
Lancaster

Part 1
Introduction

Things are always at their best in the beginning.

BLAISE PASCAL (1623–1662)

1 Applied versus Pure Psychology

Applied experimental psychology has a long and noble tradition and, apart from anything else, it is fun. It is a challenging exploration which requires the research psychologist to leave the comfort of the laboratory and venture into the outside world. The applied experimental psychologist determines to explore this world and willingly grubs amongst the slippery data which he or she will almost surely encounter. In the early stages of exploration, the applied experimentalist will attempt an investigation by direct application of the tools, techniques and methodologies borrowed from the laboratory whence they have just come. As is often the case, the standard tools issued to students are usually adequate for taking and holding the smaller, gentler, and more refined controlled studies found in the laboratory, but they are soon smashed and torn by the bigger, blacker and more uncouth situations found in the wild. Setbacks such as these often prove a very frustrating experience for the applied novitiate and repel many whose faith and commitment are not steadfast. But for those who realize and accept that the world will not be faced down solely on the terms dictated by the academician, and that its own terms must also be considered but without compromising the honour and integrity of the discipline, then success is possible. This success will not be achieved, however, unless the applied experimentalist is fully prepared and he or she should not consider entering this field without the proper equipment and training just as one would not venture into the frozen wastes of Antarctica clothed in a city suit.

Given all of the above, why should any sane research psychologist choose voluntarily to stride forth into the outside world to face a life of discomfort, frustration, high risks, and even occasional harshness? Leaving the question of sanity to one side the answer is simple: the risks are high but so are the rewards. The personal rewards that is, such as the thrill that comes one day after much hard work and many setbacks when you finally uncover a good quality scientific *relationship*. These relations are the essence of science. In other words, science is a knowledge of relationships and explanations and it is for these that experimental psychologists spend their time searching. Apart from the personal reasons it is essential, for the well-being of psychology itself, that experimental psychologists carry out research in the outside world. The psychologist, Nevitt Sandford, said that '. . . unless you observe complex phenomena directly in real-life situations, you are not really going to find out much about psychology' (Canter, 1985). Sir Frederick Bartlett, erstwhile professor of psychology at Cambridge University, has also argued that too much work in the laboratory will encourage a psychologist to become narrow in outlook and that (Warr, 1971):

> . . . he will tend to get overimmersed in a terrific lot of detail about behaviour problems which he cleverly imagines for himself, and will approximate to a sort of puzzle-solving which is often extremely interesting and in a debating sense, intellectually attractive, but which leaves him revolving round and round his limited area.

It is as though a serious-minded game playing has become the norm.

Bartlett held the view that the major theoretical advances in psychology came from those laboratories interested in practical and applied problems. This view has been echoed and expanded by, among others, Professor Donald Broadbent who has argued that '. . . the applied psychologist is more likely to make major theoretical contributions than is his academic colleague' (Broadbent, 1971). This view is based much on the fact that applied research possesses an inherent realism often lacking in laboratory based studies.

Nevitt Sandford again has remarked that (Canter, 1985):

> . . . psychologists still have the task of making discoveries. If we are going to do that, we have to look at phenomena that really exist. We have to look at people as they live and we have got to go out on the streets, or into the cities, or wherever the problems are. We need not suppose that an understanding of these is merely an application of what has been discovered in the laboratory. On the contrary; new phenomena are created in a changing society such as ours, and they must be observed directly if we are going to get a scientific grasp of them.

The strength of this coupling between applied psychological research and theoretical advances is frequently overlooked. It is overlooked by many academic psychologists, by practitioners of psychology, and most of all by students of psychology. How has this situation arisen? How has it come about that the discipline of psychology has been allowed to evolve into a false dichotomy epitomized by, on the one hand the laboratory based 'pure' psychologist, and on the other the field based 'applied' psychologist? After all, the term *psychology* refers to both the academic discipline pursued by scientists and scholars, and to its implementation by practitioners in such areas as occupational, clinical, forensic and business psychology as well as related subjects such as ergonomics and human factors. So from where comes the difference? In truth, much of the cause is historical, arising from the development of science itself, which has for centuries emphasized the minor distinctions between laboratory and fieldwork, between pure and applied research, rather than the common core of theoretical advance from research and scientific experiment, be it laboratory or field based. Given that there are still distinctions between 'pure' and 'applied' psychology, it is worth spending some moments in considering a few of the major ones in further detail.

1.1 Audiences

At the most simple level, pure and applied research differ in the type of audience which they are required to serve. Pure research is directed towards a very specialized audience. In particular those who read scientific journals, while applied research has to incorporate a more general audience and often one which comprises people with little or no scientific training. Those who move to the applied side of psychology must, as a matter of course, be able to communicate technical information to non-psychologists. As a rule, pure researchers generally expect, and tend to receive, little response to their findings, whereas applied researchers will almost certainly expect some response from their audience. Indeed a lack of response can frequently suggest a failure somewhere in their project. This naturally implies that applied research is expected to lead to action of some sort. The recipient will see the research as a means to an end, rather than an end in itself.

1.2 General versus specific

Pure research frequently generates data within contrived contexts. Its aim is to produce a theory or explanation which is both general and predictable. Applied research on the other hand is seen as being concerned with some practical problem which is in need of a solution. It is still the case that the division between pure and applied research results in much applied work being conducted at the expense of any generalization of its findings. Both these approaches have their pitfalls. Firstly, there is a danger in using laboratory experiments to study artificially constrained data. This danger lies not in the laboratory itself but in the human tendency to begin generating artificial issues for study.

Secondly, there is a very real danger that the applied approach can lead to findings that are too specific for any use outside of the immediate problem domain and by anyone other than the audience to whom they were originally addressed. That is, applied work may be unable to provide any useful information to support other areas of scientific inquiry. Herein lies the fear that applied research becomes simply what Levi-Strauss (1962) called the 'science of the concrete' or bricolage.

1.3 Snobbery

The differences between pure and applied research described above are all readily understandable. What is not quite so readily understandable, except in an historical context, is the wedge which has been driven between the two dimensions of pure and applied and which, to be quite brutal about it, is called *snobbery*. It cannot be denied that a certain amount of snobbery still exists between the 'pure' and 'applied' sciences. This condition has even plagued mathematics: Kummer who was one of the greatest proponents of number theory in the 19th century is claimed to have remarked that of all his discoveries he appreciated ideal numbers most because they had not soiled themselves as yet with any practical applications. Similar remarks have also been attributed to Gauss who is alleged to have claimed that if mathematics is the queen of the sciences, then the theory of numbers is, because of its supreme uselessness, the queen of mathematics. Interestingly, this claimed uselessness for number theory no longer holds today as it is finding many practical applications.

Scientific snobbery has been acknowledged and represented for many centuries. In the play *The Virtuoso* by Thomas Shadwell (1642?–1692), the initial scene opens on a Sir Nicholas Gimcrack who is seen making frog-like swimming movements on the table in his workroom. He is asked if he ever intends to swim in the water? He replies: 'Never sir; I hate the water. I content myself with the speculative part of swimming and care not for the practical.'

If 'pure' research is seen as the realm of academicians then conversely applied research is often seen as fit only for practitioners, that is for the servants of the discipline rather than the masters or exalted handmaidens. This attitude is not helped by those applied psychologists who have had their work justly criticized by academic psychologists for lacking in experimental rigour, for poor design, and a working knowledge of psychology which is rather dated. The true applied experimental psychologist, coming from a background of scientific rigour, will not be open to such criticisms.

1.4 Long-term versus short-term research

We are plagued by having strictly limited resources for research. This scarcity has generated a continual debate about whether such resources should be directed towards long-term and possibly high-risk research endeavours or towards short-term and often low-risk research. This question of short- versus long-term research should be an independent issue. Unfortunately, it is not. In reality the long- versus short-term research debate has become interwoven into the fabric of the debate of pure versus applied research.

The issue of short- versus long-term research can be rephrased in simple terms, e.g. what problems should be investigated? Clearly, if major findings are to be had, then one must work on the major problems and it is no coincidence that many of the radical developments in psychology (and other sciences) came through the impetus of resolving major practical problems. The Second World War produced one such impulse while in peacetime the Apollo mission to land a man on the moon produced another. It is often perceived, however, that pure research concentrates on the long-term issues, usually identified by the researchers themselves, while applied research is left to tackle the more immediate short-term problems, ones which are usually selected by others.

Applied experimental psychology does not face this dilemma. While it is theory-driven it also, by its very nature, encompasses those practical issues found in the real world. It matters not to the applied experimentalist whether the solutions sought are to be found in the short or the long term. Furthermore, applied psychology has the facility to address equally those problems which are predetermined as well as pursuing whichever lines of enquiry the researchers themselves feel to be appropriate.

It is this question of *appropriate* research which is important for the applied researcher. Given limited resources who decides which line of research will be pursued? Unfortunately, many of these decisions are determined by such nebulous groups as the government, society or a particular community. The problems which these groups identify may not, as Broadbent (1971) has pointed out, be the best ones to tackle: '. . . the community as a whole is not qualified to judge the probability that research in a given field will produce tangible results.' Furthermore, some problems, no matter how altruistic, are simply beyond the scientific techniques available today.

The pressure to concentrate on short-term research at the cost of long-term enquiry is damaging to the craft of applied experimental psychology. Investigators caught in the trap of short-term research will find themselves all too quickly becoming divorced from developments in psychological theory. It is these advances in theory which underlie the whole *raison d'être* of the applied experimentalist and to which he or she should be contributing.

There is also the view that *always* working in applied and frequently short-term research can be damaging to the long-term interests of science itself. Elton Mayo, Professor of Industrial Research at Harvard University, is reported as far back as 1939 as saying that there exists

> . . . a foolish convention that institutions engaging in industrial research are expected to 'pay their way' or 'earn their keep' this means, in effect,

that any such institution, living from hand to mouth, is committed to the futility of endless repetition of some former discovery. The interesting *aperçu*, the long chance, may not be followed; both alike must be denied in order that the group may 'land another job'. This confusion of research with commercial huxtering can never prosper: the only effect is to disgust the intelligent youngster who is thus forced to abandon the question for human enlightenment.

The above section on short- versus long-term research has been introduced because it is an issue which the potential applied experimentalist will face very soon in his or her career. It pervades the real world of politics, economics, and science and it is an issue which is not likely to go away and which cannot be sidestepped.

SAQ 1
It often seems that applied psychology tends to concentrate on specific issues. There is nothing wrong with this approach in itself, but what is the drawback for psychology generally?

1.5   What makes an applied experimental psychologist?

In this section we have briefly considered the nature of applied psychological research, its joys and frustrations as well as a few of the key issues with which the study is interlinked. Applied experimental psychology is not suited to everyone's temperament, so what characteristics should the potential applied researcher possess in order to survive 'out there'? Below are listed six fundamental qualities necessary in any applied experimental psychologist. They are not listed in any particular order because they are all important, and if one is lacking then any potential applied experimentalist is going to have a very hard time of it.

Eclectic
The applied experimentalist has to be something of a polymath. He or she needs to be active in areas other than psychology. Bartlett himself said that no good psychologist should be interested only in psychology.

Practical thinking
The applied experimentalist must be able to handle theories, concepts and laboratory techniques with the same ease and facility possessed by their theoretical and academic colleagues. But more than this, they must be willing and capable of rolling up their sleeves (sometimes literally as well as metaphorically) and working alongside the professional practitioners of psychology. Put more simply, applied experimental psychologists must be able to think with their hands.

Tolerance
It is important that any applied psychologist be sufficiently broadminded to accommodate the diversity of characteristics which will be found amongst their adopted subject sample.

Integrity
To be accepted by their subjects, the applied psychologist must demonstrate a personal and professional integrity.

Endurance
Applied research places great demands on the endurance and fortitude of investigators. If these traits are weak or lacking, then the psychologist will simply not stay the course.

Sense of humour
This is absolutely essential, and make no mistake but that it will be put to the test frequently.

Finally, it is only proper that the last word, a useful reminder, should go to Frederick Bartlett:

> ... if it is true that the general, or the laboratory psychologist must be prepared to keep his problems alive by going outside the study or beyond his immediate experimental settings, it is equally true that the field psychologist must seek his executive solution with loyalty to that rigour of scientific method and that honest sense of evidence which only the study and the laboratory appear to instil.

It is this requirement to address applicable problems with the rigour of scientific methodology which the applied experimental psychologist attempts to fulfil.

Summary of section 1

1 At the end of the day, behavioural science is still lacking in knowledge about how people behave and function in real settings. It is this problem which applied experimental psychology is suited to tackle.
2 Major theoretical advances in psychology have come predominantly from applied research. The ideas for investigation must come from the real world, and the real world is rich in potential for discovery.
3 Differences between pure and applied psychology are comparatively minor, but influential. These include:
   (a) The type of audience addressed.
   (b) The timing and timetabling of research programmes.

(c) Historical: in other words, scientific snobbery.
4 The core characteristics required of anyone venturing into applied experimental psychology, include:
  (a) Ecclecticism.
  (b) Practical thinking.
  (c) Tolerance.
  (d) Integrity.
  (e) Endurance.
  (f) Sense of humour.
5 '. . . no good psychologist should be interested only in psychology'.

2   Laboratory versus the 'Real World'

2.1   Laboratory experiments and field experiments

This book is concerned with the running of behavioural experiments, not in the laboratory, but in everyday natural settings. By doing this, one is implicitly acknowledging a qualitative difference between the laboratory and, for want of a better word, the *field*. That such a difference exists is frequently acknowledged and just as frequently ignored.

It is often implied that the laboratory experiment is the only valid means of testing an hypothesis. Arguments are supported or denounced by recourse to the authority of laboratory experiments. Scientific papers and review articles cite laboratory experiments frequently to the exclusion of all other studies and at times with little or no bearing on the practical consequences of the research for everyday life. Also, one finds that much academic psychology is concerned almost exclusively with laboratory research conveniently forgetting that the original purpose of a laboratory was to demonstrate rather than to test a specific phenomenon.

That there is a role for laboratory experiments in behavioural research cannot be denied but their limitations must be acknowledged. The main problem facing both the experimentalist and theorist lies in extrapolating experimental results from the laboratory to everyday life. It is not uncommon for laboratory findings to have little or no bearing on what happens in a natural environment. For example, after all the research which has been undertaken over the years into learning, after all those experiments, journal articles and theories, has our ability to study for an examination, to learn to drive a car, or to develop a skill really improved significantly? Hammerton (1967) has remarked that there is nothing like a little acquaintance with simulators in flying training to show up the deficiencies of psychological theories of learning. Similarly, with reference to the much studied field of vigilance, Elliott (1960) has remarked: 'Wherever we have studied real military watch keeping tasks, we have achieved some results which could not have been predicted from published test data and, indeed, we have often found the published material quite misleading.'

It is this frequent failure to extrapolate successfully from the laboratory to real life that is the crux of the problem, and it is in attempting to overcome this particular problem that the field experiment comes into its own.

Consider further the differences between a laboratory setting and a field setting. The most obvious distinction (mentioned briefly in section 1.2) is that the laboratory is a contrived situation. This is not to say that it is *artificial* or any less real than other environments. For example, it can be argued that investigating certain aspects of driving behaviour in a laboratory simulation is contrived and that the findings may not be entirely applicable to driving through an actual town centre during the rush hour. Alternatively, the study could have been conducted while driving across a desert in the Middle East. Again, the results may not have a direct bearing on ordinary driving through a town centre but it can hardly be argued that the environment was artificial; on the contrary, a desert environment is all too real. Similarly, a laboratory environment, although contrived, is just as real.

There is little doubt but that a laboratory experiment possesses advantages and attractions for the experimenter: To begin with it is possible to study single discrete variables. In research there are two primary types of variable – these are known as the *independent variable* and the *dependent variable*. The independent variable is the one which is under the control of the experimenter. It is called 'independent' because the experimenter can alter the strength of the variable independently of other factors in the experiment. The dependent variable is that variable which is measured by the experimenter. The underlying assumption, of course, is that the dependent variable is somehow influenced by the independent variable. For example, an experimenter may be interested in the effect of heat on arithmetic reasoning ability. In this instance heat is the independent variable and different temperatures can be selected and manipulated by the experimenter within a thermal chamber. Arithmetic reasoning is the dependent variable and this can be measured by, for example, the number of correct answers made by the subject on a test of mental arithmetic in a given period of time.

Suppose an applied psychologist wants to test an experimental hypothesis that a firefigh-
ter's decision-making ability would be improved if he was supplied with pure oxygen
rather than air in his breathing set.
(a) What is the independent variable?
(b) What is the dependent variable?
(c) What is the predicted relationship between the independent and the dependent
     variable?

Real life, however, is rarely as simple as this and the experimenter can
frequently find his study disrupted by *internal* variables also known as
confounding variables. For example, performance on a mental arithmetic
task may depend on the amount of fluid retention in the body, or on the
rate of blood flow both of which are known to be affected by changes in
temperature. In a laboratory it is much easier to tease apart these various
factors and to study them as discrete single variables.

A laboratory study not only enables the experimenter to separate out
individual variables, but it usually allows greater precision to be brought
to bear on the variables themselves. This it does by, firstly allowing a high
degree of specificity in the operational definition and secondly, by the
ability to vary the independent variable with a high level of sensitivity and
to measure the dependent variable with much accuracy.

Furthermore, it is easier in a laboratory to control for *extraneous confounding variables*. These are the environmental variables which surround
us all our lives and which may come between the independent and
dependent variable with the possible effect of corrupting the results. Common extraneous variables include noise, variations in temperature and
light, local surroundings and so on. The laboratory environment is constant, allowing the experimenter to 'control out' many unwanted variables. Some factors which may be a nuisance but which may also be too
awkward or perhaps not really important enough to control out specifi-
cally, are allowed to roam randomly across the experimental conditions.
This randomization eliminates bias which may creep into the results and
gives the experiment its *internal validity*. Internal validity refers to the
strength of the experimental design and the confidence one has that we are
really manipulating and measuring what we *think* we are manipulating
and measuring.

The laboratory experimenter is also in the envious position of being
able to enforce a high degree of administrative control on the running of
the experiment. Much of this control is achieved through physical isolation of the experiment, the subject and the experimenter.

As can be seen, the laboratory is often used in an attempt to 'purify'
conditions under which the experiment takes place. It seeks to discover
relations between variables under conditions which are as untainted as
possible.

A study of the experimental literature will reveal that the laboratory experiment typically serves two purposes, namely, to refine or fine-tune current theories and hypotheses and to support the building of new theoretical systems. In truth, the laboratory experiment also serves to try out intuition and personal guesses, which is no bad thing in itself, and even essential for the furtherance of natural knowledge.

Despite the above strengths, the laboratory study in behavioural research is not without its drawbacks. After all, no matter how good the experiment is, it is still only a model of the real world. Consequently, it is to varying degrees imperfect. It is also possible that the variables selected in the laboratory are not necessarily the same as those in real life. It has been argued, for instance, that the very act of bringing a variable into the laboratory can change its nature (for example, Chapanis, 1967). The precision and refinement which a laboratory study can bring to bear on an experiment may be required because the variables under study are particularly weak. This in itself is not a drawback; indeed, it can be a strength; the drawback lies in the degree of relevance which such variables have for real life.

There is also one aspect of laboratory experiments which is frequently overlooked, yet it is an important one. A laboratory experiment in behavioural research involves a strong social interaction between the subject and the experimenter. This interaction may well involve physical contact and frequently the invasion of a subject's personal space. Laboratories, certainly to the uninitiated, can produce feelings of anxiety in the subject which can contribute to error variance. Perhaps a little unkindly, but not without some truth, laboratories have been described as being little more than man-sized Skinner boxes (Silvermann, 1977). Such intergroup dynamics are not confined to psychological research. Strong psycho-social links are also found in physiological and medical experiments. Hand in hand with this psycho-social scene is the fact that the subjects know that they are undertaking an experiment, although they may not know the true nature of the study.

Like the laboratory experiment, the field experiment possesses both advantages and disadvantages for the investigator:

1 The field experiment carries a high degree of *external validity*. External validity refers to the degree to which the findings of an experiment can be generalized beyond the conditions under which the experiment was run. In other words, it is a measure of how readily applicable to everyday situations are the experimental results. It also refers in part to the degree to which the subject sample represents the overall population. As a general rule the findings obtained from field experiments do possess a very high level of external validity or practical significance.

SAQ 3

From casual observation a psychologist arrives at the hypothesis that increasing the intensity of illumination beyond a certain level on a welding job will result in a decrease in the speed with which a professional welder can weld a 12 metre long octagonal weld in a fabrication yard.

As an initial study, the psychologist has 20, second-year psychology students track along an octagonal-shaped maze with a rod under different levels of illumination. He records the time taken to complete the maze while remaining within the boundaries. This study is conducted within a laboratory where light conditions are rigorously controlled. The experimental design itself is strong.

Is this study high or low on:

(a) internal validity?
(b) external validity?

2 The variables studied in field experiments will usually have stronger effects than those variables chosen for study in a laboratory. These effects can be strong enough to overcome those naturally occurring but distracting variables which can intrude on the experiment.

3 There are far more interactions in a field setting. Consequently, a field experiment lends itself more readily to investigations into the effects of complex interactions or patterns of behaviour.

4 Field experiments are well suited to both testing theory and to resolving practical problems.

5 If the design of the field experiment can match the rigour of the laboratory experiment then statements of relationships between variables become very powerful.

It may not now come as a surprise to discover that field experiments also possess some drawbacks for the experimenter:

1 The experimental variables under consideration may be rather 'messy'. That is, they may not have quite the degree of precision or accuracy which the experimenter would have desired. This is not always the case but equally it is not uncommon. This is not to say that the variables are themselves corrupt or contaminated but that their manipulation and measurement may be more difficult than those in a laboratory and that care needs to be exerted in interpreting the results. In particular, measures of the dependent variable may tend to be rather crude.

2 Along with the experimental variables, many extraneous variables have to be accepted into the study. It is not always a simple matter to control out unwanted variables. There is frequently much random noise present. As more variables are accepted into the study the size of the effect on the experimental variable becomes relatively smaller and may even become engulfed completely.

3 It is the case that stimuli in real life tend to be non-random. This may well present a problem with randomization and in particular with the

control of independent variables. These problems, however, are rarely insurmountable and the practical reality is much more encouraging.

4 The experimenter may be unable to bring as much administrative control to bear on the running of the experiment as he or she would often have preferred.

It can be readily seen that both laboratory and field experiments possess advantages and disadvantages in more or less equal measure.

Although the distinction between laboratory and field has been emphasized, in practice this distinction may not be all that strong. It is often a matter of degree and this lies frequently in the hands of the experimenter. It is often assumed, for example, that a field experiment is by its nature poorly controlled with difficulty in randomization of subjects and treatments. These assumptions are frequently unfounded.

The experimental design itself must be sound. There can be no deviation from this. If the design is weak or faulty then your results are likely to be corrupted and the consequent interpretation worthless. If it proves impossible to run a field experiment to a sound design then abort the study altogether. This situation occurs very rarely but when it does it is usually because its time has not yet come. You may have overreached yourself scientifically.

The art of the applied experimental psychologist lies in implementation. The ideal is to mould the experiment around the activities of the host organization without either disrupting their work, or undermining the experimental design. Most field conditions set limitations on your experiment and the experimenter's skill lies in developing the experiment as far as possible within these limitations. Certain limits are fixed rigidly, e.g. aircraft piloting procedures, engineering procedures in nuclear power plants, extreme physical environments, and so on. Some conditions are more flexible, for example, a job on a worksite could be rescheduled from the morning to the afternoon providing that it is completed within that same day. Other activities may be imposed by the organization or environment which will make no real difference to your experiment.

SAQ 4
What does this mean in practice for the applied psychologist?

The laboratory experiment is itself a powerful tool and a notable advance in scientific practice. The problem lies in thinking that all science ends in the laboratory, coupled with the belief of many researchers that their study finishes when they achieve a statistically significant result. Unfortunately, extrapolation solely from laboratory studies has been found to be poor and there is a general failure to predict real life solely from a base of laboratory material. Hilgard (1964) commenting on some

15

of the more disastrous consequences of education methods points out that many who attempted to apply psychology to education had generally taken the findings of experimental research – often on animals – and applied it directly to the classroom without proper preliminary applied testing. Generalizations from laboratory work are fraught with difficulties. The field experiment is a key pin which links theory, fine-tuned by laboratory experiments, to applications in the real world.

2.2   Field experiments and field studies

Although much of this volume is concerned with the running of field *experiments*, the field experiment like the laboratory experiment cannot exist in isolation. It is but one of a number of tools employed by researchers to unravel relationships between variables which have been discovered operating in the real world. But, how are these variables detected in the first instance? Quite simply, by observation. It is essential that the psychologist goes out and observes behaviour in natural settings. The real world is rich in the potential for discovery. At one time systematic observation in the field was the major component of all natural sciences but with the coming to dominance of the laboratory experiment natural observation has become a dying art. This is very much the position in psychology although field observation is still important in such sciences as, for example, geology and anthropology. Adopting a 'look-and-see' approach to behavioural science is not only valid but essential to the discovery of significant variables.

Detecting key variables is not always an easy task. Frequently they are not actually seen but rather 'felt'. That is, an observer develops a 'hunch' about the way a particular pattern of behaviour operates. He or she has a suspicion about the possible nature of the key variables but is uncertain about its truth. Before any further progress can be made the suspect variables have to be isolated and identified. This is the role of the field *study*.

The main distinction between a field study and a field experiment is that in a field study there is no manipulation of an independent variable and no predictions to test. Rather a field study tends to be exploratory, concerned with recognizing patterns of interrelationships and the identification of their associated variables. Consequently, many field studies are correlational in nature; that is, they search for relationships between two variables rather than manipulating one independent variable in order to measure its effect on a dependent variable. They also tend to be atheoretical. After all, it is not until a relationship has been detected and threaded back to its owner variables that an hypothesis about its mechanism can be developed. Once this has been achieved and an hypothesis specified then the investigation is passed over to the field *experiment* for testing by deliberate control and manipulation of independent variables. How might this work in real life? Consider the following case study which is not too far removed from an actual experiment.

Case study of a field study
An engineering project manager, whom you know, complains in passing about the inconsistencies in weldment reports submitted by his inspection engineers which sometimes results in as many as 40 out of every 100 welds being rejected as unreliable. This situation is proving a headache to him because a satisfactory inspection is needed to obtain a certificate of structural safety. He is also at a loss because all his inspectors are intelligent, reliable and good workers. On this particular day one weld was submitted for examination by a method known as CVI (Close Visual Inspection). Four engineers carried out a CVI independently. It was found that, although their reports agreed on a number of main points, there were inconsistencies concerning the presence or absence, position, direction and type of various defects, such as cracks in the weld. There were not many but there were enough to doubt the reliability of the reports and therefore the integrity of the structure which in turn called into question the granting of a certificate of structural safety. The project manager further remarks that this sort of thing is always happening and it is a problem.

A reasonable question at this stage is to ask what the project manager and his firm are doing about the problem? – to which a very common reply would be that they are 'living with it'. This situation is usually accepted because the underlying problem is obviously human and one cannot control the human element in a problem. This erroneous view is still frequently expressed by non-psychologists who then grudgingly accept many difficulties in their work which could be resolved by the application of some psychological 'know-how'. In this example the question is posed: which factor or factors could be influencing these inspection tasks and can these discrepancies be linked to specific psychological variables?

The first stage in the investigation, that of observation, has already taken place. Everyday experience has shown that important differences can exist between individual inspection reports of the same weld. In this example, a brief discussion with other engineers will support this observation.

The next stage for the applied psychologist involves a basic analysis of the task itself. What do inspection engineers do when carrying out a Close Visual Inspection of a weld? How do they go about it? What tools, techniques and methods do they employ? What procedures do they follow? If possible have a go at the job yourself. At least try and get a 'feel' for it. Think it through with your hands. It is during this stage that you will start to generate some intuitive guesses concerning the possible factors which may underlie the observed discrepancies. Perhaps it is simply down to job experience and that the more experienced the engineer the more accurate are his findings. Perhaps it is his previous inspection training or even the individual's visual acuity. There again the discrepancies may be due to more psychological factors such as visual search ability, target detection, spatial reasoning, mechanical reasoning, working memory and so on. Again, some hands-on experience of the task will lead you to identify the intuitively most likely candidates and to reject the least likely. This is particularly important for correlational studies because all factors must be chosen on *a priori* decisions and these decisions must be argued.

Differences in inspection reports may indeed be influenced by all of these factors, or only by a few or perhaps by none at all. At this stage, who knows? Furthermore, you have no existing theory to help you in your selection of those psychological processes which are the most likely influences. You are weaving your own psychological net and it is up to you to determine how wide you make it and where you will cast it.

You are now in a position to set up a field *study*. This is, of course, after you have obtained both permission from the host organization and cooperation from your subjects. Why do you not set up a field experiment at this stage?

In this example your field study would probably involve testing your subjects on each of your selected psychological variables and comparing their scores against a measurement of performance by each inspector on a section of weld which is known to contain defects. Once the trials are completed the weld testpiece would be subjected to thorough destructive testing which would produce an accurate master plan of defects against which the individual inspection reports can be compared for accuracy. The next step would be to run a correlation between the accuracy scores and other selected variables such as visual search ability and spatial reasoning. If we assume that you find both visual search ability and spatial reasoning are significantly correlated with inspection performance while other variables are not related to accuracy, then you are a step nearer to identifying a possible relationship and developing a hypothesis about its function which can be passed over to a *field experiment* for testing specific predictions about what variables are likely to be particularly relevant in producing good, accurate inspectors.

The field study, therefore, tends to be heuristic, realistic and exploratory in nature. The main drawback to a field study is that it cannot lay claim to controlling those variables under investigation. Field studies also tend to carry a large overhead in time, equipment and administration. Interpretation of field study data can also prove difficult – but this is where the field experiment takes over.

2.3   Impact significance – or the significance of significance

You have placed your bet and you have won. You have carried out an experiment and have come up with a result which is statistically significant. So what? In many laboratory studies this is where the investigation ends. It seems to provide a natural conclusion. The results may be submitted for publication and so enter the public domain while the researcher looks around at other areas for possible investigation. The applied experimentalist cannot leave the study at this point because the experimental findings have to be applied to the real world. Statistical significance has to be translated into real-life decisions.

It is while attempting to introduce a statistically significant result back into the real world that the psychologist can come up against the problem of what this author tends to think of as 'impact significance'. That is, how important is the result for everyday life, or for the specific problem which needs to be resolved? This question arises because of the excessive refinement which many variables undergo before experimentation and which often weakens them to the extent that they cease to have any impact on performance in the natural world.

Just how usable are statistically significant results? Consider, for example, the case of the inspection engineers cited above. Assume, on the basis of your findings, that visual search is found to play a key role in inspection accuracy. Consequently, the engineering fabrication yards introduce techniques to assist visual search on a weld (in practice this can be achieved by magnetic particle enhancement). In running a field experiment to test the effectiveness of enhancing visual search ability there is found to be a significant difference in performance with visually aided performance showing a 15% increase in inspection accuracy and reliability. That is, out of every 100 inspection trials which were carried out and of which 60 were originally accepted as being accurate and hence reliable, it is now the case that 75 out of every 100 is accepted. This produces an improvement in performance which is statistically significant, but what about its impact significance? In other words has it really had an impact on everyday performance for the engineers? The answer is, probably not. If the quality control for inspection tasks sets a standard of 90% acceptability then the inspection reports are still below standard. Nonetheless, there has been a demonstrable improvement in performance. It is a start but no more. A result has been obtained which is high on statistical significance but low on applied significance.

Take the same figures but this time refer them to instances of self-injury amongst a group of psychiatric patients. It has been found in trials that following a new form of behavioural therapy a group of patients showed a 15% reduction in instances of self-inflicted damage (e.g. hair-pulling, head-banging, scratching, biting, cutting, etc.) compared to a control group of similar patients who had not undergone the therapy and to their own behaviour prior to the therapy sessions. Statistically this result is again significant but therapeutically its impact significance is virtually non-existent. Incidents of self-injury remain commonplace and consequently, even after therapy, they are *still* patients.

If, however, a 15% increase in performance occurs within a firm of stockbrokers as a consequence of your investigation into the visual processing of VDU presented financial information then this result would not only be significant statistically but would also be high on impact significance. A 15% increase in profits in any firm is noteworthy.

The difference between statistical and impact significance comes about in part because the levels of significance commonly chosen for a test (that is, the 5% and 1% levels) are chosen by convention. A conventionally chosen level of statistical significance has no connection with the importance or impact of a result. This issue can become quite involved. It is sufficient to appreciate that for an applied experimentalist any experimental result possesses two types of significance, statistical significance (has a change taken place?) and impact significance (is this change important?)

Summary of section 2

1 There is an implicit qualitative difference between a laboratory and a field experiment which is reflected in the following factors:

   (a) *Laboratory experiment*
   Advantages
   (i)   It is possible to study single discrete variables.
   (ii) A high degree of precision, sensitivity and accuracy can be brought to bear on the experimental variables.
   (iii) Extraneous variables are more easily controlled.
   (iv) The experimenter is able to enforce relative administrative control through physical isolation.
   (v)   There is a high internal validity.
   Disadvantages
   (i)   The laboratory experiment is still only a model and consequently imperfect.
   (ii) It is possible that the variables in the laboratory are not the same as those in real life.
   (iii) The effects being studied may be weak.
   (iv) It is frequently overlooked that the laboratory experiment in behavioural research is a strong social interaction.

(v)   The subjects know that they are undertaking an experiment although they may not be aware of the true nature of the study.

(b) *Field experiments*

Advantages
(i)   There is a high degree of external validity.
(ii)   The experimental variables will usually have stronger effects than those in the laboratory. These can be strong enough to overcome naturally distracting variables.
(iii) There are far more interactions in a field setting making it appropriate to the study of complex interactions.
(iv)   Field experiments are well suited to both testing theory and to solving practical problems.
(v)   If the experimental design is robust then statements of relationships between variables become very powerful.
(vi)   The results of field experiments often possess a high level of practical significance.

Disadvantages
(i)   The experimental variables may be rather 'messy' and the dependent variables, in particular, can be rather crude.
(ii)   Many extraneous variables have to be accepted into the study. As more become accepted into the study the size of the effect on the experimental variable becomes relatively smaller.
(iii) Stimuli in real life tend to be non-random.
(iv)   Field experiments tend to operate with less administrative control than laboratory experiments.
2 The main problem lies in thinking that all science ends in the laboratory with a statistically significant result.
3 Do not neglect basic observation of natural behaviour. This is how you will seek to discover your key variables.
4 A field *study* tends to be:
(a) heuristic
(b) realistic
(c) relevant.
Its disadvantages are
(a) It does not control the variables under investigation.
(b) Incomplete randomization.
(c) Difficult interpretation of data.
(d) Large overhead in administration.
5 Significance. There are two types of significance which concern an applied experimental psychologist.
(a) statistical significance
(b) impact significance – or importance.

Part 2
Preparation and Planning

A fool . . . is a man who never tried an experiment in his life.

ERASMUS DARWIN (1731–1802)

3   *Prior Preparation*

'Prior preparation and planning prevents pretty poor performance . . .', is an army expression (somewhat cleaned up for this volume) which is applicable to many walks of life, and especially to applied experimental work. It is frequently forgotten that the success of the Apollo mission to land a man on the moon (and to bring him back again!) was due primarily to meticulous planning and preparation. It is true that the role played by technology was more glamorous, but it was also less significant.

Most students will undertake experimental research as a consequence of a *project* which has been thrust upon them, usually as part of their course work. They are expected to go away and 'think about it'; returning sometime later with a hefty but neatly presented report which has a significant result and is delivered on time. This does not always happen. Many projects are rushed to meet the deadline and suffer as a consequence often being substantially weakened or corrupted. Some students need to seek extensions to complete their work, while others find that they can meet the deadline only at the cost of diverting vitally needed resources away from other areas, such as revision time for final examinations. Any experimental project needs to be thoroughly and meticulously planned. The detail must not be neglected – there is a German proverb which says that 'the Devil is in the detail.' An experimental study has to be planned, set up, implemented, analysed and reported. Each of these steps comprise a part of an overall coherent research plan and each step should be designed to facilitate the next.

The causes of project failure are various and some of the more relevant ones are considered in more detail a little later. Meanwhile, the critical factors involved in preparing and planning for an experimental project are considered below.

Summary of section 3

1 Prior preparation and planning is essential for any experiment or project which is to stand a chance of success. All preparation must be thorough.
2 The success of a project rests more on planning and preparation than any other factor.
3 Plans must be meticulous. The Devil is in the detail.

4   Getting Started

4.1   Getting the idea

In the beginning was the idea. Well, that is not always quite true. In the
beginning was usually a project which needed to be completed as part of a
course requirement. The idea tends to come second and it is this phase
which often proves to be a major stumbling block for many. It is frequently
the case that students embarking on a project are stuck for ideas. Although
they tend to know the broad area in which they want to work or the general
line of enquiry they wish to follow, they have difficulty in specifying their
thoughts. This may be due to the simple fact that the student is still new to
the game of behavioural research and believes that whatever study they
plan must have been done already. Consequently, it is a responsibility of the
tutor or supervisor to tease the ideas out of the student.

The researcher who is embarking on an applied psychological study is
often better off than his or her laboratory-based counterpart when it comes
to seeking out ideas. They will find that experimental ideas are all around
clamouring for attention. They will not have to spend time searching for
gaps in the literature on which to work. These project ideas will usually,
but not always, take the form of investigative *problems*. Sometimes,
however, the student may spot a relationship between two diverse situations which is worthy of investigation.

The student who is really 'stuck' need only walk around outside their
psychology department to find ideas of both significance and relevance. If
the investigator can 'switch off' from the laboratory and look again at the
outside world he or she will find many meaty ideas presenting a challenge
worthy of their intellectual calibre. Students who know the field they want
to work in need not worry about being stuck with a batch of project ideas
which lie outside of their own particular areas of research interest. Those
who have an interest in a specific area of psychological research (e.g.
memory, decision-making, cognitive error, ergonomics, judgement, visual perception, physiological, social, group dynamics, and so on) will find
that problems for investigation will present themselves ready made in the
format they are seeking.

What sort of ideas can be generated from a second look at the outside
world? Consider the following: What does the choice of colours for traffic
lights tell us about how a person perceives and responds to colour; what
does their presentation sequence and duration tell us about how people
make discriminations and judgements? Does driving behaviour differ significantly when approaching small country junctions compared with
urban or city junctions? If so, can this behaviour be applied to road

safety? How do people operate bank cash points? How do they *think* these points actually operate? What does this say about how people make decisions? There are noticeable differences in design between cash points of different banks and building societies, both in their physical design and in how they respond and interact with the customer (software ergonomics). Are these differences in design and operation significant? Are they important? Can the layout and interaction sequence between the customer and machine be improved? From a more social perspective, how do people use these machines? How frequently? Are some used more often than others? Do people tend to take out one large cash transaction or many small lumps in a given period? What does this tell us about the system design? One recent study (Zwaga, 1988) looked at the behaviour of people who used ticket vending machines on the Washington Metro. The study looked, in particular, at how information could be presented to the user and what actions they performed based on the information. Still on social dynamics, is it true that people walk faster in cities than they do in suburban and country areas? If so, is there a relationship between walking speed and population density? What does this tell us about group and environmental behaviour? Back to motor vehicles, why is there always one spark plug or critical bolt which can only be removed with the greatest difficulty and a 'special tool'? Why, when rebuilding the engine, are there always a couple of parts left over? What does that tell us about human perception, working and spatial memory? Can our knowledge of these areas of cognition and perception improve engineering design? What strategies do the 'old hands' in garages employ? What do these strategies tell us about human learning? And elsewhere; does piped music in supermarkets really have an effect on people's shopping behaviour? What can welders tell us about skilled motor learning and eye/hand coordination that we have not learned from the classic student maze trails?

Sport is another fruitful area of research which can also be fun. Many students perform some sport or recreation from free-fall parachuting (what causes 'ground rush' and why are some people more susceptible to it than others?) to darts (eye/hand coordination, weight estimation); weight training (body perception) to card games (subjective probability); orienteering (fatigue, perception, decision-making and reasoning) to ballet dancing (proprioception, kinaesthetics) and so on.

This approach carries an impressive imprimatur in the form of Professor S.C. Bartlett who held the Chair of Experimental Psychology at Cambridge University, and who spent a great deal of rather pleasurable time studying skilled performance in the game of cricket, and in particular what went to make up an efficient stroke (Bartlett, 1951). As an aside, it is worth pointing out that the knowledge gained from this work later had significance for industry in such areas as precision control and tracking (e.g. Taylor, 1960).

Consider also the payoff from this particular approach; a final-year undergraduate project can often involve around six months work. What burning ambitions, avocations or personal interests does the student have which he or she would *willingly* invest six months of their lives in and find it rewarding? It may be a sport, or a hobby or a general field of interest or perhaps a planned step in the student's career. One student, for example, decided that he wanted to enter the financial sector after graduating. Consequently, his research project led him to investigate data presentation and decision-making in a firm of stockbrokers. There is no activity in which psychology cannot gain a foothold. To re-quote Professor Bartlett '. . . no good psychologist should be interested only in psychology'.

SAQ 5
What is one of the best ways for discovering fruitful ideas for applied research?

Some recent undergraduate and postgraduate student projects may serve as an example of what can be achieved in the applied area. These include a study of perceptual, motor and cognitive performance underwater (involving both sport and professional divers). A study carried out at a major firm of stockbrokers into the cognitive and perceptual factors used by brokers and dealers in processing screen-presented financial information. A study of personality and its physiological correlates among people within high risk occupations (this included sample groups of subjects drawn from, among others, army paratroopers, combat divers, and professional Formula-one racing car drivers). A study of different physical conditions on pilot performance; an experimental study into cognitive, perceptual and procedural errors among drivers involved in road accidents; a study into prospective memory amongst operators in a nuclear power plant; the effects of alcohol and caffeine on maritime navigation skills; personality and perception amongst junior and senior police officers; the effects of heat and humidity on military skills in the field; a comparison of the effectiveness of three types of post-coronary treatment in a general hospital; a study of value perception following a three-month African expedition. One student, for her final year psychology project, primed an experiment to run at over 16000 feet in the Everest region of the Himalaya.

If, after all this, you are still having difficulty finding an idea to work on just spend some time in a pub, or in a queue at a supermarket check-out or post-office counter, or in a canteen or at a road junction, airport, building-site, fishing harbour, tower-block, hill-top or indeed anywhere at all. Keep your eyes and ears open, your mouth closed and a notebook and pencil to hand; you will not lack for ideas afterwards.

Finally, a word of caution about ideas themselves. Ideas are very elusive and fleeting and have a tendency to come at the most inopportune of moments. Unless these ideas are nailed down as soon as they arrive they will disappear altogether. Always carry a small pocket notebook in which to jot them down before they can escape and cultivate the habit of collecting ideas like some people collect stamps.

Summary of section 4.1

1 The seeds of ideas for research projects are all around. Problems are clamouring for attention throughout our own daily lives and the lives of others.
2 Many problems requiring investigation are not trivial, but present challenges worthy of the intellectual calibre of the products of our universities, polytechnics and colleges.
3 Behavioural research can be conducted anywhere. The limitations are only those of your imagination. There is no work, no activity, society, organization or environment which is not ripe for fruitful psychological research.

4.2   The aim

Let us assume that you now have the germ of an experimental idea. Also, that you have at least the basic background knowledge of the subject from the psychological standpoint and that you have identified your target group of subjects (mechanics, bank clerks, golfers, pilots, nurses, springboard divers, unemployed former executives or whomever).

The next stage is to *plan* your project. Do this as soon as you can. Do *not* leave starting your project until later, hoping perhaps for time or inspiration, but get stuck into it as soon as possible. A drop of blood and sweat invested early prevents an awful lot of tears later. Many people have a natural tendency to assume that everything will be all right in the end. It rarely is.

Experimental planning requires methodical and disciplined thinking and, as a practising applied psychologist, you will need to bring a high degree of precision to bear on the experimental plan. This is not as imposing a task as it may seem. To start with, simply plan out the whole project as a chart on one sheet of paper. (There are more advanced techniques and tools available to assist you in planning, such as the Gantt chart, flow chart, critical path analysis, etc. and some of these are considered in more detail in section 6.) The main function of a planning chart is to force you to marshal your thoughts and to think your project through methodically.

Begin with the *aim*. What question(s) is your project seeking to answer? Crystallizing the aim is the most critical part of any experimental project. The difficulties frequently encountered by students part way through their project can be traced back to a poorly defined aim. Write down the aim of your experiment and express it in one sentence only, preferably beginning with the preposition 'To . . .' thus:

> *Aim:* To determine whether experienced welders employ different perceptual–motor strategies than inexperienced welders.
>
> *Aim:* To identify the perceptual factors underlying the inspection of electronic circuit boards.
>
> *Aim:* To determine whether memory for motor movement is impaired at altitude.
>
> *Aim:* To identify the key information elements needed by investment analysts to make effective decisions.

The aim is usually the first hurdle the experimenter faces. If the aim cannot be presented in one sentence then the project has not been thought through sufficiently. The tendency is to believe that you know what you are doing but your ideas are not yet firm enough to build on. The problem and, therefore, the project, is still fuzzy. Before any investigation can proceed the problem to be investigated must be bounded. Often problems are simply too vague or too general to be tackled. They are, if you will, too soft, so that the tools currently available to psychological researchers are unable to obtain a grip. In order to make the problem amenable to their tools it must first be captured, bounded and defined. Furthermore, it must be defined quite narrowly. Establishing the aim is a key process in bounding the problem.

Sometimes you may find that your project has attracted more than one aim. Do not join these together. For example:

> *Aim:* To identify the key factors in financial decision-making ability and to see whether decision-making is affected by colour coding screens presenting financial data and whether there are significant individual differences between successful analysts and those who are not so successful.

You may indeed be investigating all of these factors in your project but operationally this type of conjoined aim will only cause conflict and confusion. The project aim could be re-written as:

> *Aim:* To identify key factors in decision-making ability among effective investment analysts.

Once this is done you can tackle the *objective* for each experiment separately. In this way you will avoid internal conflict while still keeping the whole project together.

SAQ 6

What is the key positive indicator and the key negative indicator in written experimental aim?

For a project to be successful the aim must be established well in advance and then kept constantly in view. Failure to do this will result in the researcher capturing too much information and being forced to handle too many factors at one time. Furthermore, a vaguely defined aim increases the temptation to modify the experiment when it is only part-way through. If this happens you will end up with the worst of two worlds: firstly, the study will become overloaded with information and, secondly, it will prove virtually impossible to retrieve all the necessary data retrospectively. Once the aim is established then – and only then – is it possible to organize the gathering of data systematically.

There are three further points concerning the aim which are worth considering:

- Firstly, you are initially writing it down for yourself not for anyone else. This is to help you focus your thoughts on the *operational* side of the experiment. You may wish to include a statement of the aim in the project report or experimental paper, but that is for later.
- Secondly, your aim is *not* your hypothesis. Whereas the hypothesis is a starting point for the experiment, the aim is a starting point for the project.
- Thirdly, once the aim is written down on paper it is committed and the project will become established in your own mind.

Interestingly, you will now find that matters relevant to your project will suddenly start appearing without your seeming to seek them out. Odd points in conversation and snatches of material in journals, papers and magazines will now claim your attention whereas before you would have overlooked them. Browsing through libraries (often fun but frequently fruitless) will now become more productive. Questions, operational and experimental, will leap to mind wanting answers.

Finally, if you are unable to express your aim in simple writing then seek help from your tutor or supervisor otherwise it will be very difficult indeed taking your project further.

Summary of section 4.2

1 Your project will stand or fall on its *aim*.
2 The *aim* serves to bound and define the problem under investigation.
3 The *aim* should begin with the preposition 'To . . .'.
4 Do not confuse the *experimental aim* with the *project aim*.
5 Have only *one project aim*.

4.3   The plan

The plan must simulate your project as it will actually exist in practice. It must, however, be as simple as you can possibly make it. Remember KISS – Keep It Simple Stupid. As a rule of thumb remember that if you cannot, at this stage, plan your thoughts on one side of paper, then they are overcomplicated.

The main reason for planning is to determine what resources will be needed to answer the experimental question, and in what order these resources are to be applied. For example, how many subjects will be needed for each condition? Where will you find them? What equipment will be needed? Planning will also enable the cost of resources (including time) to be estimated and provide a means of monitoring the development of the project. Do not expect your first plan to work straight away. It will usually require much reworking and refinement before it becomes finally and fully functional. Techniques and methods for planning are considered in section 6.

A word of warning: some students, particularly those of a scientific bent, will find that planning itself becomes a sufficiently exciting and absorbing activity to dominate the project. This is especially true once students have come to grips with various planning tools such as network diagrams. The result is that an essentially simple project becomes overplanned and that far more time and effort is surrendered to the planning stage than to the project itself. Concomitantly, the plan ends up being so detailed, so choked with interlinking activities that it becomes ossified and brittle. It will certainly prove unworkable in practice. The Americans often refer to this condition as *analysis paralysis*.

A project, especially one concerned with applied behavioural science, cannot be run by numbers alone. At some point there must be contact with human beings and human beings live in the real world. The plan is to ensure that when the time comes for contact to be made all will run smoothly.

Summary of section 4.3

1 The *plan* will simulate your project as it will actually perform in practice.
2 Keep the plan simple (KISS). Avoid overplanning and the risk of 'analysis paralysis'.
3 Remember, that at some stage your plan must engage the real world.

4.4   Choosing a sample

A *random sample* is one which has been chosen without any bias. Only a random sample will truly permit deductions about the variability of a population to be made. Randomization allows you to mathematically relate the experimental sample to the overall population. In an ideal world all samples would be drawn randomly. Unfortunately – or fortunately depending on your point of view – this is not an ideal world and random samples are not always there for the taking. This difficulty is especially pronounced in the field of applied psychology.

In simple random sampling, each subject and condition is allocated a number. These numbers then present themselves to the experimenter in such a way that each has exactly the same chance of being chosen. This may be achieved by putting each number into a revolving drum and drawing out one number after the other. This method is commonly used to allocate teams in sporting competitions. In simple terms, it is a lottery. With large samples, tables of random numbers can be used or alternatively a computerized random number generator. Many of today's computers (and even a few pocket calculators) possess random number generators which can be used either directly or to generate tables of random numbers. This random number generator function is usually called RAND, RAND (Y) or sometimes RANSEED.

When discussing a random sample it should be noted that the term 'random' refers to the process of selection rather than to any property of the sample itself.

Although subject randomization can be achieved with little difficulty in the setting of a psychological laboratory it is far more difficult to achieve in a field setting. This is often due to operational constraints. For example, you may not be able to test individuals nominated by your random procedure, but may instead have to work with individuals who are detailed off to you by a supervisor. One way to overcome this problem is to randomize your conditions rather than your subjects. If you are testing under three conditions (say, three different light intensities in a visual-inspection task) then the condition (a given light intensity) is randomly selected for each subject rather than the subject being selected for the condition. It can be argued that this is the same thing. It is not quite the same but it amounts to the same which is the important point. Essentially, it ceases to be a sampling problem and becomes instead an assignment problem.

Difficulties can arise however, when you are testing subjects who have been allocated to you in groups. Testing groups of people rather than individuals tends to make your experiment operationally more effective but can raise problems for randomization. If unwanted effects do creep in because of operational reasons, then all is not necessarily lost. There are techniques (usually mathematical) which can, if not always eliminate, then certainly identify and contain unwanted variance. These techniques, however, are not recommended for the novitiate.

Such is the nature of applied experimental psychology that there will be occasions when, even with the best will in the world, it will not be possible to allocate subjects and conditions in a truly random fashion. Fortunately, there are associated methods of sampling which are also valid. These are known as *stratified sampling, cluster (multi-stage) sampling, systematic (equal-interval) sampling, quota sampling, attribute sampling, panel sampling* and *'accidental' sampling*. Each of these is considered in more detail below.

4.4.1   Stratified sampling

This form of sampling is used when, although it is not possible to test the whole population, all levels or strata of the population must be represented in the sample. On a simple level, this may mean equal numbers of male and female subjects being present in the sample, or it may require the representation of every rank in a county police force. Clearly, in the latter case, normal random sampling could well exclude certain ranks altogether. Once the population has been divided into predetermined strata, the subjects chosen within each strata are selected by normal randomization methods. It is obvious, in the example above, that there will be only one chief constable in your sample. However, it is possible to select the police force itself by random means from all those in the country.

4.4.2   Cluster sampling

Cluster sampling, or multi-stage sampling, is a method of reducing large-scale sampling to manageable forms by carrying out random samples at successively lower stages of the population. If you need to find a sample of schoolchildren for an experiment you could obtain the names of all the children in the country of school age and select them by techniques of randomization. Such an approach is rarely practical. Instead, you begin by selecting at random a local education authority. Next you select, also by randomization techniques, a school within that authority, then a class within that school and finally the pupils themselves.

4.4.3   Systematic sampling

Systematic, or equal-interval sampling, can be very useful in situations where it is not operationally possible to select every person or condition by random methods. The technique of systematic sampling involves selecting say, every fifth or tenth or whatever number person who appears in your population. The population in question may comprise, for example, train passengers, bank customers, pedestrians, sport spectators, farmers at a cattle market, and so on. Now, deciding to select every fifth person would not by itself be random. Such a decision is predetermined and consequently no-one else in the sample would have a chance of being accepted. It is a requirement that every member of the population has an equal chance of being selected at the outset. A degree of randomness can be incorporated into the sample by selecting the first number at random. If you are sampling subjects at intervals of five and your random number generator gives you a three, then your first subject will be the eighth one to appear (5 + 3 = 8), followed thereafter by subjects number 13, 18, 23, 28 . . . etc. Equally, if your random number were nine then you would test subjects 14, 19, 24, 29 . . . etc.

4.4.4   Quota sampling

There are occasions when a person who has been chosen at random for your sample cannot or will not take part in the study. Essentially, quota sampling says that in this case you may legitimately substitute someone else from the population. This is on the basis that one engineer, insurance clerk, long-distance lorry driver, toolmaker, shopper, deep-sea fisherman or whomever, is as good as any other. There is, of course, a risk of experimenter bias creeping into the sample with this method and it should only be used within certain limits. Occasional substitutions are allowed, routine ones are not. If there is a large-scale refusal to take part in your study then you need to go back to first principles and ask yourself why this resistance exists.

Another means of reducing experimenter bias is to introduce a degree of stratification into the sample, such that the individual who is to be substituted meets criteria similar to that shown by the randomly-selected subject. You might insist, for example, that the substitute be the same age, sex, come from the same social background and possess the same level of educational attainment as the original subject. You will find that most quota samples possess some degree of stratification.

A variation of quota sampling (sometimes known as *purposive sampling*) is used to select members of a population known by the experimenter to possess specific properties or characteristics which are suitable for certain research purposes. These people are considered by the experimenter to be 'typical' of the population he or she is investigating.

4.4.5   Attribute sampling

Attribute sampling is a method of selecting people for an experiment according to a particular attribute which they possess. This attribute may be one of experimental relevance or of experimenter convenience. An example of the former would be the selection of subjects who are red–green colour blind for a visual-search experiment involving the colour coding of screen-presented information. An example of a convenience attribute can be found in that classic of epidemiology – the field trial of the Salk poliomyelitis vaccine. In this study, conducted in America in 1954, over one million schoolchildren took part as subjects. Their attribute was that they were all in the second year at school. In the United Kingdom a major longitudinal study is underway to follow a group of people throughout their lives, from birth to death. Their particular attribute is that they were all born on one particular day.

4.4.6   Panel sampling
Panel sampling is most frequently encountered in market surveys, but it also has applications in experimental studies. Panel sampling involves establishing an initial sample, by any of the above methods, then using the selected people to obtain results on several occasions. This is particularly useful in longitudinal studies and epidemiological research, where you may wish to monitor trends over a period of time. Any changes are more readily identifiable with this form of sampling than with several independent samples.

Panel sampling does have some drawbacks. It is not always easy to persuade people to be re-tested on a number of occasions. There tends also to be a rather high drop-out rate amongst the subjects once the initial flush of enthusiasm for the study has waned, and replacements then have to be found. It is possible to overcome this effect of attrition by recruiting a much larger number of subjects than you really need in the first place thus compensating for the effects of natural wastage. In other words, if your analysis requires a minimum of 20 subjects you might recruit an initial pool of 40 people which will provide a safety margin of 50%. This will carry a concomitant overhead in resources which must be planned for.

4.4.7   'Accidental' sampling
It can be argued that 'accidental' sampling is not true sampling at all. As a technique it is hard to defend. It is also the most common method employed in both pure and applied psychology. Accidental sampling means, quite simply, that you take as your subjects whoever happens to be at hand. A class of children drawn from the nearest school; the clerks or customers at your local bank (after all, you do know the manager so it can make the initial approach a bit easier); experienced welders? Well there is a fabrication factory just over the bridge, and so on. Nor must it be forgotten that it is 'accidental' sampling which leads to so much psychological research being carried out on psychology students.

Accidental samples can be used providing they are coupled with a heavy dose of common-sense and healthy suspicion in the analysis and interpretation of the data which they yield. They are to be considered as a last resort only.

Finally, randomization of subjects and conditions is a fundamental process in behavioural research. Without randomization the viability of your findings may be called into question. Randomization is a major advance in scientific method. It is not a synonym for accidental, haphazard or willy-nilly; nor does it mean 'regular' which is sometimes implied in common speech. If your subjects or conditions are selected randomly then you must state how this was achieved, for example, by the use of random number tables or generator. If your subjects or conditions were not selected randomly, then again state firstly, why they were not so selected and secondly, what alternative method of sampling was employed.

SAQ 7
You are conducting a study into cognitive dissonance between ministers of the Christian religion and non-believers. Given that you have limited resources and that there are substantially different Christian sects, what form of sampling could you use to ensure that your sample is representative?

(a) random   (e) quota
(b) stratified   (f) attribute
(c) cluster   (g) panel
(d) systematic   (h) accidental

SAQ 8
You are interested in misperception in human performance which results in motor-vehicle accidents. In the initial phase of your investigation you wish to carry out a field survey amongst people involved in motor accidents. Your project receives the support of a major motor insurance company who possesses a list of all their clients involved in accidents during the past 12 months. For reasons of confidentiality they will not pass on their list to you but say that they will forward your questionnaire to every 50th person on their list. What is the problem with this method, and what do you advise?

Summary of section 4.4

1 Randomization
   (a) The technique of randomization is a major advance in scientific method. Randomization does not mean haphazard, accidental or regular.
   (b) Methods for randomizing subjects and conditions commonly involves 'lotteries', random number tables or a computer-based random-number generator.
2 Sampling
   In field research it is frequently impossible to allocate subjects and conditions in a truly random fashion. In such circumstances alternative methods of sampling are possible. These include the following:

   • stratified sampling
   • cluster sampling

- systematic sampling
- quota sampling
- attribute sampling
- panel sampling
- 'accidental' sampling.

4.5   *Project failure*

There is failure, and there is *failure*. The first type of failure is absolute. The project has collapsed completely even to the extent where, for example, the award of a university degree itself may be in jeopardy. Such an extreme situation.has certainly happened although, fortunately at the undergraduate level, this is rare. The second type of failure is relative. It occurs when a project has not met its full potential and may often require the experimenter to carry out a salvage operation in an attempt to recover the project to a level which at best is often barely survivable. These 'salvage jobs' are far more prevalent than many people appreciate or perhaps wish to acknowledge. It is, therefore, worth taking some time out to briefly consider the factors which underlie project failure.

Failure, of course, is not confined to student experiments. A survey of 1403 major projects in 135 organizations carried out by the Massachusetts Institute of Technology (MIT) found that only 60% of these projects were considered successful. An estimated 11% were complete write-offs and the remaining 29% were salvage jobs; that is, they could be lived with, but no more.

Previous work (see for example, Waters, 1988) has found that three conditions are necessary for a project to succeed. These are:

- Commitment
- Control
- Communication.

If any of these conditions is missing then your project or experiment will almost certainly fail. Unfortunately, it is still possible for a project to fail if all three conditions are present, but the probability of failure, and especially total failure, is greatly reduced.

4.5.1   *Commitment*
Commitment is shown by the willingness with which a person puts his or her resources into your project. This includes not only yourself but your supervisor, your subjects, the personnel in the host organization, your assistants, and so on. Resources will include time, energy, money, equipment and people. Commitment *must* come from the top (usually your supervisor) and from the front (yourself) and it must pervade the whole

project. Clearly if you do not commit yourself to your own experiment then you can hardly expect to engender commitment in anyone else. The judicious use of project management tools and techniques can help to raise commitment by showing that your plan has been well thought through. They show the plan to be achievable.

4.5.2 Control

Control means ensuring that everyone in your project or experiment is doing the right thing, in the right place, at the right time, and in the right order. In essence, control is your paper plan in action.

4.5.3 Communication

Communication should pervade your project or experiment as water pervades a sponge. There is no excuse for anyone involved in your study (from supervisor to subject) to say that they do not know what is happening. Students are frequently astonished that their ideas and assumptions, which they took for common knowledge, are in reality known to very few. Poor communication produces a loss of clarity which can often result in conflict. As an applied experimental psychologist you will find that the requirement for communication at all levels soon becomes very apparent as does the need to communicate technical matters to non-psychologists.

Summary of section 4.5

1 It is a fact that too many projects are neither successes nor absolute failures. They can be lived with, but no more.
2 Three conditions are necessary for a successful project:
   (i)   Commitment
   (ii) Control
   (iii) Communication
   If any of these is missing, the project will not succeed.

4.6 Plan failure

In the previous section the key factors which can lead to the failure of a project have been identified. This section will consider some of the problems which can beset your planning. Far too often plans can look good on paper but fail to match up to their practical implementation. There are various reasons for this failure and the more common ones are discussed below.

4.6.1 Poor experimental definition

This arises when you are still not clear in your own mind precisely what you are doing. It is analogous to a ship at sea with an excellent satellite navigation system on board but the captain is not sure to which port he wants to sail. It is for this reason that so much emphasis was given previously to writing down the aim of the experiment. It helps you to narrowly define the experiment and only then can planning really begin.

4.6.2 Optimism

Or perhaps more correctly *over*-optimism. Students, especially at the beginning of a project, tend to be very optimistic people. They hold the view that all will work out well in the end. Consequently, they tend either to not plan at all, plan very loosely or most commonly, leave all planning to the very last minute. Too many students leave their projects until the 13th hour.

Over-optimism is usually the result of inexperience. This inexperience breeds the notion that everything will go as it has been planned for the simple reason that it *ought* to do so. This fallacy usually shows its mark on exceptionally unrealistic estimations of time and costs. Unfortunately, optimism and denial tend to go hand in hand. Optimism is excellent while it is tempered with realism, otherwise it becomes dangerous, and it is very noticeable that optimism quickly turns sour when the plan starts to go wrong. Once this happens your research project will become no more than a chore and the fun will be lost altogether.

4.6.3 Distraction

It is all too easy for an experimenter to become distracted from the main line of enquiry. During the literature search and the initial setting up of the experiment many tempting but peripheral ideas are uncovered which issue a siren call to the experimenter to re-direct his or her resources towards resolving, rather than adhering rigidly to the declared aim of the project. These temptations should be brought firmly under control. This is not to say that they should be ignored, far from it, but that they should be addressed at a more convenient time and on your terms only.

There is also the danger that an experimenter can become distracted by the tools themselves. They may, for example, become too absorbed in the techniques of project planning or of computer applications such that more time and effort is spent on these supporting activities than in carrying out the project itself.

4.6.4 Effort

One of the reasons for over-optimism is the frequent use of a warped estimating formula: namely, that effort = progress. It is not only assumed that effort means progress but that this assumption works on a simple 1:1 basis. This produces an intuitively comforting belief that to double the progress of a project all one has to do is double the effort. Consequently, a project can be completed in half the time with twice the effort. This is the implicit defence against a project which looks like running over time. This, of course, flies in the face of all that is known about systems and the way they function. It matters not if they be human or engineering systems.

It is true that a few activities can be speeded up by merely putting in more effort but many others cannot. A plan is designed to prepare the way for the smooth running of an experiment on the day, but no amount of planning will allow it to be rushed through. Similarly, a word processor can only print a 300-page dissertation at a given rate. No amount of intense concentration on behalf of the author is going to produce the document any faster.

While the usual consequence of increased effort is an initial and appreciable increase in progress this increase soon falls victim to the law of diminishing returns. Further effort will frequently result in a decrease in progress as more errors creep into the schedule. Fewer of these errors are detected or corrected, reserve time (see p. 43) is exhausted and activities come into conflict. This, of course, is the inverted-U curve so familiar to behavioural scientists.

4.6.5   Over-planning
Some people will find a tendency for their plan to dominate the project or experiment. This manifests itself as an unhealthy involvement in too much detail, which in turn stifles flexibility and creativity, spawns bureaucracy and leads to the condition mentioned above of 'analysis paralysis'. Over-planning is a subtle trap and scientists appear to be more prone than many to being lured into it.

4.6.6   Under-planning
Under-planning, on the other hand, will usually show itself in the omission of important activities, items or resources. This again is often down to inexperience in the running of field experiments. Should you intend to continue as an applied experimental psychologist you will find it fruitful to keep a record of your field experiences which will aid you in your planning. The most useful document for this is your site diary which is discussed further in section 16.2. It becomes very clear at this stage that the probationer applied psychologist is serving a genuine apprenticeship in his or her craft.

4.6.7   Time
It is important to ensure that your project can be completed in the time available. A lack of appreciation of time is the most common bugbear of

projects and experiments. It is the cause of more experiments going awry, and of more projects needing to be salvaged than probably all other causes put together. Time can become a problem because of an over-optimistic assumption that all will work out well in the end. It can become a problem because the plan and resources have been poorly estimated. Time can be a problem simply because an experiment is being run in the field rather than in a laboratory. It is worth remembering a simple rule of thumb: it *always* takes longer to run an experiment in the field than in a laboratory. Life and the scientific literature abound with examples, here are but two:

- During the flight of *Gemini II*, astronaut Richard Gordon was to go outside the capsule and tie the *Gemini II* capsule to an Agena rocket with a 33 metre (100 foot) cord. As Gordon said (Anon., 1966):

  All I had done in 30 seconds in the laboratory turned out to be a monumental task of about 30 minutes. It was easy to perform in training, but it was really work in space.

- One research psychologist used divers to study context dependent memory in two different environments; on the surface and underwater. He reports (Godden, 1975):

  Medical fitness, weather conditions, equipment failure and aborted dives all played their part in turning a four-day laboratory schedule into a two-week open water marathon.

Not only does it take longer to run an experiment in the field than in a laboratory, but it also takes much longer to set it up in the first place. It is also clearly observable that the more people involved in a given activity, the longer it will take to accomplish. Do take time out for rehearsals before committing yourself to the field. Time is a valuable resource in its own right which your project badly needs. Give it all you can. There are two types of time which will have a direct bearing on your project: *lost time* and *reserve time*.

4.6.7.1   Lost time   Lost time can occur when your plan becomes too divorced from reality. It occurs when people fall ill; when your subjects are not available because a crisis has occurred in another department; when there is a sudden transport strike; when the person in the host organization to whom you have been told to report has not been told to expect you, and much much more. Holidays seem to be a particular problem and it is well worth obtaining a copy of your subjects' holiday rota. Although this works well for block leave, it is not really effective for the many occasional days which crop up. This is an important factor should your experiment require the re-testing of people. Lay your planned time scale against a calendar and see how it looks; you will not be the first to have scheduled an experiment for 25 December. You must not ignore lost time.

The problem with lost time is that it will not be noticeable in its early stages. After all, the deadline is way in the future and, of course, can you not always make up the lost day with some other day? Rarely is this possible. What happens instead is *slippage*. Slippage in a project or experiment is subtle and insidious. It worms its way into the very foundations of your plan corrupting the design and ruining the experiment. Slippage occurs in small doses and consequently is rarely detected until the project deadline looms up, and by then it is too late.

Dr Frederick Brooks was a Senior Project Manager at IBM for many years. In his time he has handled a number of extremely complex, expensive and time-consuming engineering and computer projects. He has also made a personal study of those factors underlying the management of computer projects (see for example Brooks, 1982). He has summed up slippage very succinctly: 'How do projects get to be a year late? . . . One day at a time.'

4.6.7.2   Reserve time   Reserve time is the time you have captured for your project from various quarters. It comprises the time you have grabbed by getting stuck into the programme as early as possible; the time you have managed to save by careful and methodical planning and preparation; the bucketfuls of time you have saved by making effective contingency plans; the slivers of time you have collected by working on your project in those odd spare minutes that pepper the normal working day.

You need reserve time to pay off the debt incurred through lost time. If you have little or no reserve time then at best your project will overrun, at worst it will crash.

In the initial planning stage it is useful to work out on paper how long the experimental project will take . . . then multiply it by three!

4.6.8   Failure to monitor
Sometimes plans are drawn up with genuine care and honesty but then they are simply neglected and left to gather dust in a desk drawer. Plans are there as a tool to assist you in monitoring the progress of your experiment. This allows you to keep control of your project. Failure to monitor allows the real world to spring sudden surprises on the project which presents the experimenter with an urgency which he or she may deal with at the expense of the important. Your project should be monitored regularly and frequently. This way you can detect any natural divergence from the plan and take effective and timely remedial action. It is through the cracks left by a failure to continually monitor that slippage will creep into your project.

When deciding upon your area of interest for a research project, especially if the project has to be submitted within a very short period, say for a degree assessment, remember that you will be severely constrained by two important resources: time and money. Especially your own. By all means be adventurous in your research, but be realistic.

SAQ 9
What is the most common underlying cause of experiments and projects going wrong?

Summary of section 4.6

1 A research plan can fail for various reasons. The more frequent causes are:
 (a) *Poor experimental definition:* you are not yet clear in your own mind what you are about.
 (b) *Optimism:* more correctly, over-optimism, which is born of inexperience.
 (c) *Distraction:* you become distracted by tempting but peripheral ideas which come across your path while setting up the study, or by the tools themselves such as computers.
 (d) *Effort:* beware the fake assumption that effort = progress. It is not a direct 1:1 relationship.
 (e) *Over-planning:* this is a temptation which needs to be guarded against. It spawns bureaucracy and leads to analysis paralysis.
 (f) *Under-planning:* this is another consequence of inexperience.
 (g) *Time:* it *always* takes longer to run an experiment in the field than in a laboratory. There are two types of functional time:
   Lost time: which occurs when your plan and reality become too divorced.
   Reserve time: which you have actively saved by careful and realistic planning.
 (h) *Failure to monitor:* where a plan, once drawn up, is forgotten or ignored. This allows the real world to spring some nasty surprises.
2 How does your project get to miss the deadline? . . . One day at a time.

5   Specifications

Once your plan has been established, the next stage is to draw up a functional specification. The plan itself is concerned with what you are going to do and when you are going to do it, while the specification is concerned with how you are going to do it. As with the plan, the main strength of the specification is that it forces you to think the programme through in a methodical manner. A functional specification brings a discipline to your experiment.

Formal specifications and requirement documents are commonplace in other areas of science and engineering but appear to be little taught in the behavioural sciences. There is, however, a common form of specification called a *research proposal* which describes the project in rather general terms, tending to take a broad overview of the whole project instead of dealing with the details. This is, of course, as it should be. Apart from anything else, the audiences are different for a proposal and a technical specification. A more detailed proposal is sometimes referred to as a *protocol*.

The experimental or functional specification is a technical document which describes what you are going to do and how you are going to do it. This specification is comparable to the architect's drawings, the engineer's blueprint, or the computer system's manual. Although, for the most part, the technical specification is for your own use, it should be written to a standard where someone else with a working knowledge of experimental procedures can use it to run your experiment independently.

At first this may seem rather horrendous. After all you surely have more than enough paperwork to cope with without adding to it. Fortunately, in practice this is not quite so harsh a task to achieve. At least it is easy providing your thoughts are reasonably clear, and if they are not, then drawing up a specification will help to put them in order. A functional specification also serves to resolve conflict and to reduce the number of queries which can arise once the experiment is under way. These queries may be sufficiently critical to bring down the experiment altogether. Furthermore, the cost in resources of resolving a query once the experiment is under way is many times that of resolving it during the specification or pilot study stage. It is important to emphasize the role of a functional specification. This book is not concerned with the more usual two-hour classroom practical experiment but rather with psychology experiments that are to run outside of the laboratory under field conditions. These will undoubtedly have claimed a lot of commitment from your subjects and support personnel and you owe it to these people to have planned meticulously and to have prepared thoroughly. This is what a specification helps you to achieve.

Much of the information required in a specification can be presented as a list of short (one or two sentences) statements. The type of information which should be included is considered under the following headings:

TITLE:
This is the title of the project.

AIM: (see section 4.2).

RATIONALE (*or* OVERVIEW):

This is a simple statement of what you are planning and the reasons behind your experiment. This may vary from a single paragraph to a couple of pages and maybe more in a multi-experiment project. It is essentially a general description of the experiment. Much of the information contained here will find its way into the INTRODUCTION section of your project report.

SPECIFICATION:

Hypothesis: state clearly your experimental hypothesis.

Independent variable: what it is and how it is to be applied.

Dependent variable: what it is and how you are to measure it. If there is more than one dependent variable then detail each one separately.

Controlling factors: what factors do you need to control to avoid contaminating your experiment? List them. What means do you propose to use to control them?

Subjects: type and description, from what population is your subject sample to be drawn, minimum number required, total number planned for, etc.

Units of measurement: this is what you will be collecting from your subjects, e.g. milliseconds, distance moved, personality test score, catecholamine levels, pupil dilation, number of correct responses in a given time, and so on. How many measurements will you be taking?

Tests and/or measuring instruments: this should include brief details of all your test equipment.

OPERATION:

This is the 'how to' part of the specification. For example, how are you to brief your subjects? What instructions are you to use? How are your subjects to be tested? Will they be tested individually, in pairs, small groups, or altogether? What instructions will be given to your subjects about the experiment? How will the test be administered? How will the experimental apparatus run? How will the data be recorded? Will they be collected in a notebook, on a graph printout, or will they perhaps be captured directly by computer?

EQUIPMENT:

List *all* the equipment and materials that you will need; from an eight-channel physiological monitoring system with remote telemetry to pencils, rubbers and stopwatches.

ANALYSIS:

Explain in detail how you propose to analyse the data. This should include the types of statistical tests, with a brief note explaining why you have chosen these tests over others. What assumptions have you made (e.g. comparable variance)? What do you do if your assumptions are falsified (e.g. the laws of variance are violated in your samples)?

You should also detail any physical analyses which need to be carried out (e.g., chemical analysis for catecholamines, blood cell count, body

46

weight and so on). Sometimes such analyses may be particularly complex requiring specialist or technical support in which case it will usually suffice to simply note the type of analytical method employed, and by whom (e.g. haematocrit analysis, Dr J. Smith, University Biochemistry Department). Further details can be included in an appendix if necessary.

A sentence or two on the possible outcomes of your findings can be useful. If Null Hypothesis rejected then . . . what are the implications? If failure to reject Null Hypothesis then . . . what are the implications?

APPENDICES:

These are useful for holding specific details such as technical analyses and maps of the physical layout of the experimental location.

SAQ 10
What is the underlying purpose of preparing a project specification along the lines detailed above?

Drawing up the technical specification for your experiment may seem a bit of a chore at first sight, but it is a very useful exercise indeed. The initial effort required to outline the specification is repaid manyfold once the laboratory is forsaken and your experiment is committed to the field. Writing a technical specification for an experiment is essentially a decision-making process. Committing the experiment to paper in a structured form forces the experimenter to resolve many of these small, but crucial, issues which too often remain fuzzy. The very act of writing a specification highlights all those gaps and discrepancies in the experiment which would otherwise remain dangerously concealed like miniature land-mines. Once these decisions have been made, all that remains is for them to be communicated. You will now find that the specification is itself an excellent means of communication. It is important to remember that, once the project is underway, an applied psychologist's main duty is that of communicating, not making decisions. There is an additional advantage when it comes to writing up the experimental report, as most of the work (especially the thinking!) has already been done. Similarly, all the information which will probably be needed for a general proposal (e.g. for your host organization) is to hand.

As an aside, it is worth mentioning that writing out plans and functional specifications helps to break the habit inherent in too many students who consider experimental write-ups and reports as no more than a nuisance; something to be tacked on to the end of an experiment rather as an afterthought. This habit is unfortunately instilled during school days. Experimental reports and papers are of course the definitive means by which research findings are conveyed into the public domain and this carries much responsibility for the author.

The specification is a *technical* document and it exists to help you. It will also, of course, be of immense help to your supervisor and fellow collaborators. On this point, it is a useful practice to have the specification officially 'signed-off' by your supervisor showing that he or she both understands and agrees with the programme of work as detailed in the document. The specification need not, indeed should not, be an awe-inspiring document. Keep it short and concise, curt even, but ensure that all necessary information is contained therein. The functional specification will evolve as your plan develops. It may, for example, require some major modifications following your pilot studies. That is after all one of the reasons for running pilot studies. One note of encouragement: the writing of technical specifications for experiments does become easier with practice.

Summary of section 5

1 A functional specification details how your experiment is to be run. It is a technical document comparable to an engineer's blueprint.
2 A functional specification serves to identify gaps in your thinking, resolve conflict, eliminate queries, force decisions and aid communication.
3 A proposed format for a specification would include the following sections:

- Title
- Aim
- Rationale (or overview)
- Specification
- Operation
- Equipment
- Analysis
- Appendices

4 Once a specification is completed, the experimenter is relieved of most of the decision-making. All that remains is to run the experiment and to *communicate*.

6   Pilot Studies

A question often raised by students is whether or not to run a pilot study of their experiment. This question is really a non-starter. Given that a pilot study can be considered as a 'throw-away' experiment, the question now is, do you plan a throw-away experiment or will you risk throwing away your actual experiment? Remember that your experimental design, no matter how meticulous, is never so thorough as to guarantee success. Although pilot studies are designed to be thrown away, they are never trivial. They allow you the comfort of modifying your design or procedure before finally committing yourself, and your experiment, to the field where any experimental errors or procedural blunders will stand out with an embarrassing boldness, for all to see and ponder.

A pilot study is analogous to a model or a pilot plant. No one, in constructing large-scale engineering systems, moves straight from the drawing board to a full-blown operational system. It is a recipe for disaster. Engineers and the like know only too well that scaling-up is rarely on a one-to-one basis. For our purpose, the pilot study is in effect a model of the actual field experiment. Because it is a model it is not expected to be perfect. Indeed, as a model, it will not be perfect.

Running a pilot study of the experiment requires a little patience but the returns can be high. Serious problems or flaws, especially on the operational and design side, can be identified and corrected in good time while the administrative procedures can be rehearsed and refined.

A pilot study is run for three main reasons:

- Firstly, to highlight any experimental anomalies, e.g. floor or ceiling effects in your tests.
- Secondly, to ensure that the experiment is administratively and operationally possible. In other words, that when it comes to the day you can actually do the job.
- Thirdly, there are occasions when results obtained from a pilot study may support your argument for running the main study. This is often useful when it comes to seeking permission from external host organizations to run your experiment on their premises.

Finally, it is much less expensive in time, money and effort to correct a faulty experiment during the pilot stage than it ever is once the experiment and resources have been committed to the field. It is also much less embarrassing. Ultimately, of course, a pilot study can tell you very quickly if your main study will be a pointless waste of time.

SAQ 11
How many pilot studies should be run?

Complementing the pilot study are two useful techniques. These are known as the *walkthrough* and *mock analysis*, and will be considered below.

6.1 Walkthrough

Before conducting a pilot study it is often a useful exercise for the experimenter to carry out a 'walkthrough' of the experiment. A walkthrough is

49

essentially an experiment without subjects. It is a pen-and-paper exercise, with the experimenter taking on all the roles: setting up apparatus, briefing subjects, administering tests, logging data, and so on. It is at this stage that a functional check of all the test equipment should be carried out. A walkthrough can be conducted alone or with an assistant.

6.2   Mock analysis

Far too often have the corridors of various psychology departments echoed to such enthusiastic cries as, '. . . I've collected all my data, now how do I analyse it [*sic*]?' Such a gross lack of foresight often leads to a salvage operation being needed on the project. On too many occasions have students launched themselves wholeheartedly into projects, collecting stacks of data during their trials which at the end of the day they are unable to analyse. In desperation they will usually throw much of their data away or will try to enforce inappropriate tests in an attempt to recover at least something from their hard-won data grubbing exercise. This situation occurs most commonly among students who are beginning to become more adventurous in their experiments. They start to construct designs with multiple conditions, cross nestings and so on.

To avoid the above problems ever arising, simply take a sheet of paper and draw up a table or set of tables for the *type* of data that you will be collecting from your subjects, e.g. test scores, time intervals, heart rate, distances covered, etc. Do this for each test condition. Next, fill in these tables with mock data of the type you expect to obtain. For example, if you are measuring perceptual speed in milliseconds, draw up a table and fill in a column with data in milliseconds. Now try and analyse this data. You may well be in for a surprise. Apart from determining whether or not the data can be analysed, mock analysis frequently highlights changes needed to strengthen the experimental design and may even help to crystallize or question the underlying assumptions of the hypothesis. Clearly, it is better that this be done before commencing any experimental trials. Remember, any data that are to be logged must be structured. Once a structure has been imposed on the data, the means of analysis become more discernible.

In conclusion, the question every student should now be asking is: why *shouldn't* I run a pilot study?

Time in the field is at a premium. There is no second chance. Design – walkthrough – mock analysis – pilot study – experiment.

Summary of section 6

1 The question every student should ask is: 'Why *shouldn't* I run a pilot study?'
2 A pilot study is a model of the experiment. It serves to:
   (a) Highlight any experimental anomalies.
   (b) Ensure that the experiment is administratively and operationally possible.
   (c) Provide collateral for running the main experiment.
   It can also show very quickly whether or not the main experiment will be worthwhile or a waste of time.
3 Complementing a pilot study are:
   (a) The *walkthrough*. This is a pen-and-paper experiment without subjects.
   (b) The *mock analysis*. This is a rehearsal of the analysis phase. It is a practise run of the statistics.
4 The time you are able to spend in the field is always at a premium. You will not have a second chance.

7   *Obtaining Permission*

In order to carry out any experiment in the field you will, in almost all cases, need to obtain permission from some authoritative body. When considering from where to obtain permission, it is worth noting that it never comes from committees or boards but always from individuals. The key is to identify that individual. You will soon be surprised at the number of people in senior positions whose role is to implement company policies which they do not understand nor have ever questioned. These people are of use, but can take up much of your time.

Contrary to much popular belief among psychology students, obtaining the necessary permission to run applied experimental studies at outside locations, using the indigenous subject population, is not too difficult. This even applies to some areas which people tend to think of as being automatically out of bounds, such as the armed services or police force. Student projects have been run using, for example, army paratroopers, fighter pilots and serving police officers as subjects. There are of course exceptions, and the experimenter must expect to have his or her request for subjects turned down politely but firmly.

Many commercial, business and industrial organizations will also be willing to assist you if they can. Again it is often a case of contacting the right person. On one occasion the author managed to set up a set of experiments involving the visual processing of screen presented financial information within a major firm of stockbrokers simply on one five-minute telephone call. Incidentally, this call was merely to find out who should be approached in the first place. In this instance, the right person was reached at the right time.

Rarely is it so simple. For example, one project, concerned with the study of skilled motor learning in everyday life, required the use of qualified and experienced (coded) welders at their usual place of work, which in this instance was a construction site for a tunnel. The question now was, who should be contacted for permission to run the experimental trials? The boss of the site firm was a good start, but the welders turned out to be sub-contracted by another firm of engineers, which in turn had been contracted out by an independent authority who was ultimately responsible for the tunnel. Some background work was obviously needed in order to find the most effective way around the system. But it was done and a successful and interesting study was accomplished. The author once ran a series of experimental psychology experiments in the middle of the North Sea, requiring the separate and simultaneous permission of a major diving contractor, the diving superintendent, the oil company representative, the ship's master and the oil platform safety officer for *each* experimental trial. And this was after asking the subjects themselves if they would like to cooperate!

Sometimes of course you will come up against a dead end. This may be because no one is quite sure what to do with you, or you may have approached them at just the wrong moment (e.g. when people are being laid off), or the only person with the appropriate authority is a genuinely cantankerous and all round unpleasant sort. You will soon discover that many more people have the authority to say 'no' to something than have the authority to say 'yes'. It is not uncommon for these people to veto something merely to exercise this authority.

The more common response is a qualified 'yes'. That is, the person you have approached is happy in principle for you to go ahead with your experiment, but they themselves may need to have it authorized by their own superior. The difficulties can really start when the authority has to be obtained from different people, sometimes different departments which may even be in different parts of the country. This has certainly happened with one very large organization where an application had to be cleared, not only through the target section itself, but through four other sections in four widely different parts of the United Kingdom. One authorizing section it turned out was completely unknown to the target section. It took 18 months for clearance to come through, but once through it was virtually a *carte blanche* thereafter. This type of deadlock may have arisen because entrance into the organization was at too low a level for what was needed. One solution is to go higher up the organization rather than across and around it. This must be done diplomatically as it will entail going over the head of your immediate contact. Before taking this sort of action, discuss it with your host first. He or she will probably pave the way for you anyway. When planning your project you must include time for a decison-making knock-on effect. As your request and proposal are bounced along the line each individual in that line will need time to make their own decision. You will have to calculate the number of 'in-trays' you need to pass through.

Before approaching any business, industry or organization, it is worthwhile obtaining some general background information on the firm's structure, organization product or service and the names of the key personnel. Most reference libraries will store some company information, especially of the larger organizations; and the *Kompass* business directories, for example, are very useful. A telephone call or letter to the company's sales or marketing department can usually elicit some useful brochures and other material.

Once the initial approach has been made, you will normally be required to submit a project proposal to a named contact for further consideration. This may be done in writing or in person or both. At this stage you *must* be fully prepared and crystal clear on what the aim of your experiment is, what you want to do, when, and how, right down to the last detail. Too many students have gone away to organizations unprepared, sometimes with only a whisper of an idea, and have been summarily shot down. This can wreak havoc on both morale and public relations. There is no excuse for being unprepared at this stage. Naturally, some of the procedural detail will have to wait until you know what, if anything, is going to be made available to you by the host organization.

It is now that the effort put into your proposal or functional specification pays off. If you have established your experimental aim, drawn up a functional specification and run a pilot study, you should have little difficulty at this stage. A little rewriting may be required to ensure your proposal is simple, concise and avoids jargon. If you must use jargon then make sure the terminology is explained as simply as possible, and as early on in the report as possible.

Have no illusions about what you are asking for. You are asking for this person to put his or her resources (especially their time and workforce) at your disposal and, in most cases, to do so voluntarily. Nothing comes free. Consider: if your experiment requires 30 minutes to run per subject and you test 16 people, that is the equivalent to one man-day lost to the host organization. So you must spell your requirements out. The person in charge may or may not be interested in your experiment *per se*, but they will certainly be interested in knowing what they must commit to your project. The person you are liaising with will want to know for example:

- Why you need to use these people in particular as subjects?
- Why not another group? This is a very important question and you must be clear in your own mind why you need these people rather than others for your experiment.
- The number of subjects you will need?
- How much time will be needed to run your tasks (can they be tested in a group or must it be individually)?
- What *precisely* are the tests that you will be running?
- Will it be a one-off testing session or will you need to return for repeat trials? And will these be the same as before or will they be different?
- Will you need to test your subjects in a specified order or as they come? Sometimes, of course, you will not have much choice in this matter.
- What facilities or equipment will you need to have on-site (if any)? For example, a private room for testing, electrical powerpoints, sink and running water, table and chairs, and so on.
- Sometimes you will be asked (quite rightly) about your own qualifications and experience. If any queries are raised then a letter of accreditation from your university or college will usually be sufficient to satisfy the questioner. Your supervisor or tutor should be able to arrange this.
- And of course, what is in it for the host organization or their people? This particular question may be raised directly but frequently it is implied. If your work is of benefit to your host or their organization in any way (and it should be) then they are usually far more interested. This is only to be expected, so spell out any possible benefits.

Answer the above questions simply and honestly, and on no account try to bluff. Obtaining permission to run an experiment is rarely difficult and once it has been granted you will find that most people will put themselves out to help you.

So far concentration has been on obtaining permission to run your experiments in business, industrial, commercial, public sector, and similar organizations. This is simply because if you are after specific groups of subjects then these are the communities where you will find them. There are of course other relevant groups which can be most fruitful for behavioural research. In a previous example, welders were cited as being excellent subjects for a study on sensory-motor performance. In that instance the normal psychology maze-tracking experiment was replaced with a welding or weldment tracking experiment. Incidentally, this was an exciting experiment to run because the results had direct relevance to the sample group and everyone was happy to give up their time to take part. This was one sensory-motor study, for another it might be more appropriate to consider, say, a team of sportsmen or women (e.g. highboard divers, fencers, or ballet dancers) as more suitable subjects. On one occasion, as a student, the author conducted an experiment into the effects of fatigue on aspects of visual perception which involved the local rugby club running, for what now seems an awful long time, around the old West Ham Football Ground. They claimed to find the session both demanding and a welcome change from their normal training routine. Would their enthusiasm have remained intact had they been required to repeat the session?

Some studies, of course, can be carried out without any external permission being required at all. Much can be learned, for example, about human behaviour from experiments or studies conducted in shopping precincts, at road junctions or on railway platforms, in city centres, and so on. Another field frequently overlooked but also exciting for behavioural research is one comprising the different physical environments: hot, cold, high, low, wet, dry, humid, clammy, rocky, slushy, muddy and so on. The inside of the cockpit of an aeroplane or a modern air conditioned computer building is just as much an 'environment' as the middle of a large city or the middle of a desert. As mentioned briefly before, one student managed to tie her experiment on cognition into an expedition to Everest.

Whatever the field you choose to work in, the only requirement is that the study be truly *applied experimental psychology*.

Summary of section 7

1 Contrary to much popular belief, obtaining permission to run applied experiments at outside locations is not difficult providing it is approached sensibly.
2 Committees do not make decisions   individuals do. You must track down the person with the authority to say 'yes' or 'no' to your proposal. Especially the one who can say 'yes'.
3 Before you approach any organization, ensure that you are clear on what you will be asking for. It also helps to have a basic background knowledge of the structure and function of the organization in question.
4 Do not underestimate the cost of your study to the host organization.

8   Site Reconnaissance

'Time spent in reconnaissance is never wasted', is an old military adage which has much relevance to the running of psychological experiments in natural setttings. Wherever possible an advanced visit should be paid to the location where you intend to run the experiment, be it a suite of offices, a manufacturing plant, a road junction, a stock broking trading room, an air-traffic control tower or even a piece of waste ground. In many cases you will be invited to visit the site to discuss your project, and that is an excellent opportunity for a preliminary look around. Never visit a worksite without knowing precisely the questions you want answered. After all, you are not a tourist – you are there to do a job.

An essential tool for any site reconnaissance is a pocket notebook. This is not only for taking notes but should also serve as an *aide-mémoire* in which you have jotted a list of items which may need to be clarified or confirmed on-site. There are always some outstanding points and they can be very easily overlooked unless they are noted. For example, will you need power points, if so, how many and what type? Will you need extension cables? Will you need access to a water supply and/or washbasins? What is the ambient noise level and will this cause a problem? Is the lighting, heating, humidity, etc. acceptable, is it adjustable, does it matter? Is there a suitable storeroom for your equipment? What about parking facilities and security? One multinational organization classified its car park as a secure area and visitors were not allowed within the compound. A pass, complete with personal photograph, had to be issued before the car park could be used. This naturally took time. Prepare for it. Quite often, on initial site visits, you will meet more people than you can usually recall later on. Make a note of their names, positions and other relevant details. Try to do this discretely but not furtively. Incidentally, you will be surprised at how easy it is to visit a workplace and speak to a number of people without actually speaking to, or even seeing, one of your potential subjects. Make a point of trying to speak to a few of your subject pool during the visit, they will come to recognize your face and word will soon get around.

Sketch-maps of site areas can be very useful if you need to design a physical layout for your experiment. Cameras, especially those of the Polaroid type, can be very useful tools in site reconnaissance. There also exist some very handy-sized cameras which fit neatly into a jacket or shirt pocket. On no account assume you can take photographs. Always ask permission beforehand as some field settings may be classified as restricted areas usually for reasons of security, either defence or commercial. Also, and it must be said, you might just come across one or two places whose work practices may not be in total harmony with various factory and government regulations. They may get a bit twitchy if they see their deficiencies being permanently and unequivocally recorded on film, especially by an outsider.

Whether your experimental setting is indoors or out of doors you must check and double-check the site layout to ensure that it is physically impossible to conduct your experiment. Do not be too concerned should you need to scurry under desks clutching a tapemeasure and notebook – the chances are that your hosts will expect this of you!

Work through the checklist in your notebook as systematically as possible and if any points are obscure then clarify them. Whenever possible
always see for yourself what the situation is like. You cannot trust anyone
to do this for you – not because they are dishonest but simply because
other people always assume things differently from you. For example, one
student was repeatedly assured that the site portakabin allocated to him
would have an electric power supply which he needed for some of his
equipment. And so it did. But what he had not been told was that the
generator supplying his electricity was immediately outside the cabin
window and he had to almost shout to get his instructions over to his
subjects. Another student was told that all his subjects were on one site
but in two locations. It was only when he was part way through the first
set of trials that he discovered that the locations were half a mile apart,
and that there was no across-site access. The work site was much larger
than he had assumed, and to travel from one team to the other between
trials involved a five-mile round trip on each occasion.

All reconnaissance visits should be written up in detail in the site diary
(see section 17.2 on the site diary).

Summary of section 8

1 Time spent in reconnaissance is never, ever wasted.
2 Before visiting a worksite make sure you know precisely what information you need to take back. What questions do you need to ask?
   What facilities do you need to see?
3 A pocket notebook and pencil is compulsory. A small camera is option-
   al but often useful.
4 Always see things for yourself.

9   Matériel

Matériel – in other words, your equipment. This includes both the experimental apparatus or material and the gear you will need to actually admin-
ister the project.

An equipment manifest or checklist is essential otherwise you *will*
forget items. Most checklists will have four headings: *experimental; administration; personal; miscellaneous*. Each of these headings may be on

a separate page. The types of item subsumed under each heading might include the following:

Experimental

20 × MMPI test booklets
30 × MMPI answer sheets
  1 × MMPI instructor manual
  1 × PC512 computer
  1 × PC512 keyboard
  1 × Application software
  1 × Application software
    back-up

1 × Application software manual
1 × Kohs Blocks (set of 9)
1 × Kohs Blocks test pattern
   booklets
1 × Timer
Data record chart
Data record notebook
Instructions sheet

Administration

Road map
Company address list
Company site map
3 × Functional specifications

Portable notice board
Memo pads
30 × Pencils (HB)
30 × Pencils (2B)

Personal

3 × Hard hats
3 × Safety goggles

3 × Overalls
Cold weather gear

Miscellaneous

10 mm × 50 mm polypropylene rope
Paint brushes
Brewing kit (Do not knock it!)

Ensure that all necessary spares are included on the list. More than one experiment has had to be postponed for want of a new bulb, fuse, battery, pencil sharpener etc.

The checklist should preferably be typewritten and there should be at least one set of duplicates made. All the equipment should fit into a secure container or containers for safety, security and transportation. Large brief-cases will often do perfectly well for much of the equipment and surplus amunition boxes can be very useful.

If you decide to continue in the field of applied experimental psychology then you are strongly advised to start building your own personal emergency kit pack. This will contain those small but universally essential items such as:

Sellotape	Fuse wire
Pocket stapler	Drawing pins (put these in an old
Pencil sharpener	35mm film canister)
Pocket stopwatch	Bulldog clips
Watchmakers' screwdrivers	Tape measure
Miniature electrical kit	Needles and thread
Pliers	First-aid kit
Small scissors	String or cord
Pocket knife (invaluable,	Bottle opener
especially the Swiss Army type)	Two–three pin plug converter
Paper clips	

These are the small and frequently overlooked items which, when it comes to plugging holes and keeping your experiment running, are worth their weight in gold. You will be surprised at just how frequently you will have recourse to this particular piece of kit to bale your experiment out of a tight spot. It also takes up surprisingly little room and can usually be fitted into a large plastic sandwich box. There is one applied psychologist who claims that the most important piece of equipment in his emergency pack is his old school biology dissecting kit.

It is worth mentioning one further point about equipment and applied experimental psychology. Scientific equipment has been known to malfunction, always disrupting and sometimes destroying an experiment. All equipment should be checked and overhauled regularly, and at least once on the day before you deploy into the field. Equipment failure does not need to be dramatic to be disruptive: the author can recall one student experiment which had to be aborted because of a broken rubber strap and two other student experiments because their marker pencils would not mark in the wet. In all these instances the experiments were conducted out of doors (literally in the field) and required a large amount of organization and logistic control by the experimenters, and much commitment from the subjects. In such cases the outcome can be more than just embarrassment for the experimenter. (Incidentally, the difficulty of finding marker pens or pencils which will write when damp is a perennial problem in certain types of experimental environment and one which ought to be resolved in this day and age.)

Much of the equipment used in experimental field trials, particularly by students, is standard laboratory equipment or 'off-the-shelf' psychological tests. In many cases this is perfectly adequate. After all, most pen-and-paper personality tests, for example, can be completed just as well in the factory, or bank, or on board a ship as in the psychological laboratory. Other equipment will not function either adequately or at all outside of the laboratory without some form of modification. Sometimes this modification can be quite a simple process such as laminating the pen and paper test in plastic or constructing a perspex housing for a finger oscillator recorder, or on one occasion, constructing a pursuit rotor within a heavy-duty sealed metal housing for use during sensory-motor performance trials in a particularly hostile environment.

There are occasions when experimental equipment will have to be specially designed and constructed. This may not be a particularly difficult or complex task but it does depend on the knowledge, skills, finance and technical support available to you. If your own department cannot help at any point (usually for reasons of funding but sometimes because your request is rather exceptional), then scour the local environment. The author managed to construct three experimental test rigs for an engineering psychology experiment from good quality 'oddments' obtained almost gratis from a metal fabrication company. Other manufacturing companies have also donated various items over the years for research purposes. To many such firms you will be seen rather as a latterday Autolycus, a mere '. . . snapper-up of unconsidered trifles' (*The Winter's Tale* iv(iii)) and they will often be intrigued by what you are about. There is little doubt that the mark of a true applied experimental psychologist is the well-thumbed copy of *Yellow Pages* in the bookcase.

Do be spare in your approaches though. Many companies are willing to help you but do not abuse their generosity. And do not forget a note of thanks after the event.

Summary of section 9

1 Applied experimental psychology involves the use of more *matériel* than is found in laboratory studies. All equipment should be identified on a checklist under following headings:
   ● Experimental
   ● Administration
   ● Personal
   ● Miscellaneous
2 It may be necessary to modify standard psychology equipment for field use, or even to construct new items from scratch.
3 Construct your own experimental emergency pack to rescue your experiment when the equipment starts to go wrong.

10   Logistics

Logistics is concerned with the supply and movement of equipment and people. It deals with the procurement of equipment and its storage in reserve until needed. It covers the bringing together of the *right* equipment and material in the *right* order, the *right* quantity, the *right* condition, to the *right* people, in the *right* place at the *right* time.

In small experiments logistic control is relatively simple. Much of the equipment can be taken more or less 'off the shelf', stored in the psychology department until needed, then packed up and taken to the test site. In many instances your equipment will be transported by motor vehicle or simply by hand in a large briefcase. If you are working out of doors then it may be necessary to portage your gear. This possibility should be borne in mind during the planning stage, e.g. how many people will you need for the carry? Over what distance? One student's psychology experiment took place on Helvelyn in the Lake District. This, as can be imagined, involved a significant amount of equipment portage.

The logistic requirement for much larger, multi-project research programmes has become a research objective in its own right. This topic lies outside the scope of this book but the interested reader is referred to texts in the area of operations research.

Summary of section 10

1 Logistics is an important element in any study conducted in a field or natural setting.
2 Logistics is concerned with the supply and movement of people and equipment to the *right* place, at the *right* time, in the *right* quantity, *right* condition and *right* order.
3 Logistics must be incorporated into your project plan.

11   Contingency Planning

Some form of contingency planning is essential if you are simply to survive 'out there', let alone bring back some useful data. Contingency planning usually means planning for uncertainty. It is not easy to do and requires a rare combination of foresight with hindsight. The keywords are *'what if . . .?'* and you should go through your plan with these in mind.

- *What if* – you cannot test your subjects in the exact order you had planned? Does it matter to your data collection or experimental design? What is the minimum number of subjects needed? How many should you test?
- *What if* – you cannot re-test all your subjects on the follow-up trials? Do you still have enough subjects for your analysis? If not, what can you do to avert aborting the study completely. This is a very serious risk in applied research.
- *What if* – one specific piece of test apparatus fails to function on the day? Do you abort? Can you postpone? Can you still obtain worthwhile data from the other tests?

Below are some of the more prosaic reasons for experimental sessions becoming bogged down (*Note:* these incidents have all happened for real):

- *What if* – the key to the room which you have been allocated by the host organization has been put somewhere safe for you? No one can remember where.
- *What if* – the person in authority at the host organization to whom you have been told to report on the day (a) has never heard of you, (b) expected you tomorrow/yesterday or (c) is dead?
- *What if* – the particular part of the worksite you wanted, and where your equipment is already set up, is flooded?
- *What if* – the electricians are on strike?
- *What if* – you turn up on-site to be told that you cannot have your subjects after all?
- *What if* – your colleague (never *you* of course!) has brought the correct test but the wrong response sheets?

One of the main contingency aids to saving your project, if not necessarily a specific experiment, is to build up your reserve time as early as possible (see section 4.6, on plan failure).

' Much is learnt from experience of course but a 'what if . . .' approach helps to forestall many of the major problems. One student, for her final-year psychology project, studied the effects of heat and humidity on military skills in soldiers. This was a field study conducted outside the UK with the British Army. Part way through the study, Iraq invaded Kuwait and she lost one of her two groups of control subjects overnight. Anything can happen. When plans do go awry then log the details and compile a list of the causes along with your remedial actions. This is best done in your site diary which is discussed in section 16.2 (p. 77). It is often the glaringly simple or obvious factors which will trip you up. Do compile a list of these problems although you, of course, will never make the same mistake twice (!) you must give some thought to those others who will be tentatively following in your footsteps – 'out there'.

Summary of section 11

1 What if . . .

12   *Psychological 'Tools'*

Research is a craft and, like any other, an apprenticeship must be served and the tools of the trade mastered. The most obvious tools of the psychological profession are, of course, the equipment and hardware with which one frequently comes into contact in psychological laboratories: stopwatch, pen-and-paper tests, tachistoscope, ECG, tape measure, video camera, finger oscillator, tape recorder, lists of nonsense syllables, pursuit rotors, galvanic skin response recorders, and so on.

The not so obvious 'tools' are the tests of analyses and the various statistical techniques and methods.* Also your experimental designs and procedures are equally recognizable as being tools of the psychologist's trade and, as a practising applied experimental psychologist, you will need to master these instruments. You will need to know which tool to select and when to use it to craft your experiment from the raw material to hand.

As well as tools, the applied experimentalist needs to develop skills. He or she must be able to communicate their experiment clearly to many people, not least their subjects who will come from a myriad of backgrounds. This must be done effectively and without being patronizing. The experimenter must be able to gain the confidence of both his hosts and subjects. This will undoubtedly require background research into a completely new walk of life and, more importantly, it will require the patience to prepare as thoroughly as possible.

---

* These statistical techniques are covered in detail in a companion volume in this series: *Learning to Use Statistical Tests in Psychology* by Judith Greene and Manuela D'Oliveira (1990) published by Open University Press.

Summary of section 12

1 Research is a craft and the applied experimental psychologist needs to serve an apprenticeship to master the tools, techniques and skills of the craft.
2 This apprenticeship can be a long one and it will not be achieved without a certain amount of effort and application by the apprentice.

Part 3
In the Field

Go as far as you can see. Then you will be able to see further.
THOMAS CARLYLE (1795–1881)

13   Administration

Experimental administration is a much neglected and often despised part of research. After all, experiments are *run*, not administered! Students, in particular, often fail to appreciate the consequences of poor administration for the outcome of an experiment. Those who have had their fingers burnt amongst the embers of a crashed experiment learn very quickly the importance of careful and thorough administrative techniques. Nonetheless, it still frequently occurs that inexperienced experimenters will turn up at a given site or host organization with a letter of permission in one hand, a bag of psychological tests in the other and the vain hope of being able to go straight in and run their experiment. This is courting disaster in the extreme. Administration must be planned for and one of the first things you will need to establish is an on-site room from where you can run your experiment.

13.1   A psychological 'ops room'

It is important for the smooth running of your field experiment that you establish within the host company or organization suitable temporary but dedicated accommodation from which to organize your trials. Remember also that the primary function of this room is administration and not experimentation. If you like, it can be considered as a psychological operations room from which your experiments will be launched. Most host organizations will be happy to accommodate you in this matter and a few will have arranged it automatically. Frequently however, you will have to find the room for yourself; this is often because the host organization itself is unaware of precisely how many rooms it actually possesses, where they are located, which are in use, and which are vacant. There has been more than one occasion where the author has successfully run an experiment from a room of whose existence the people in the organization were completely unaware. Your admin room need not be a formal office, indeed any little cubby-hole somewhere on site is usually perfectly adequate. The main functions of this room are to allow you somewhere to store your equipment, to log data as they arrive, to have messages posted, to monitor experiments, to drink tea and, occasionally, to hide. There also appears to be a psychological booster in having a secondary office. On the one hand it enables the experimenter to feel less cut off from his or her own department, while on the other hand enabling them to feel less alienated from the people within the organization in which they are working.

Your admin room may or may not be furnished but do not expect it to be. If your experiment is being run primarily out of doors then you will, of course, supply your own basic furniture, e.g. folding chairs, foldaway worktop, stand-up noticeboards, etc.

Whether your admin room doubles as a testing room for subjects will depend entirely upon the nature of your experiment. If you do need a separate testing room you must make this clear to the host organization well in advance of your experiment; if only because such a need will not have occurred to them in the first place. It is also worth reminding the organization of your requirements closer to the day of the trials because by that time they will either have forgotten, or the people you have been in contact with will have moved to new locations, posts or jobs, or the room will have been pre-booked by someone else. This is quite a common and infuriating occurrence. The author has had the experience of being turned out of a room pre-designated for experimental trials on three separate occasions within three days because the same room had been booked by other people. The person responsible for room allocations apologized on each occasion for the disruption and on each occasion promised it would not happen again!

Most rooms on-site will be perfectly adequate for your experimental purposes. There are some types of room, however, which you must be wary of and some which you must avoid altogether. Those to be avoided at all costs include canteens (always unsuitable) and workers' rest rooms. Employees often lay great territorial claims on their recreational rooms and they are used by the staff at many odd moments. You are most likely to be offered canteens and rest rooms by those organizations whose activities are primarily out of doors, e.g. building sites, construction yards, dock yards, etc. First-aid rooms can be useful, or not, depending upon circumstances but they are always worth considering. They are often unoccupied, clean and carry an air of efficiency and professionalism which can be infectious. However, to some people (i.e. your subjects) first-aid rooms can possess an unpleasant atmosphere, producing unwanted stress effects in your trials. Nonetheless, the author has used first-aid rooms to very good effect. If you are offered a first-aid room, and you do decide to use it for your studies, you must be aware of the implications: firstly, do not fill it with your clutter, secondly, be prepared and able to move out in seconds in the event of an emergency. Most work sites are dangerous places.

Administration and testing rooms are not limited by four walls and a door. You may find it worthwhile to consider other forms of accommodation, such as a converted caravan or other motor vehicle, mobile containers and even large tents, especially if your trials are to be run out of doors. In these instances you will also have to supply furniture, not only for yourself, but also for your subjects.

If your experiment will involve much equipment and paperwork and/or you will be running trials at different sites then right at the outset you need to draw up, as well as an equipment checklist, a plan or diagram of how the items are to be arranged in the room. Precisely where are the tables and chairs going to be placed? Where is the test apparatus to be located? Where do you need to have the data log sheets positioned? Do you need screens or a noticeboard? Where are these to be positioned? A predetermined layout diagram relieves you of the trouble of trying to work out where everything should go in each room, and explains the layout simply to anyone else involved in planning the accommodation or assisting in setting it up.

13.2   The importance and problems of breaks

In the previous section you were warned off using canteens and rest rooms as administration and testing rooms for your experiments. The main reason for this is that these types of rooms are prone to being invaded at very short notice by large numbers of people who wish to use them for their designated purpose – that is, to have a break. Most of your subjects will have a routine of sorts for tea and lunch breaks. Sometimes these are rigidly enforced, usually but not always by the unions. In some organizations the break can take on the status of a company ritual. In other jobs the breaks are more flexible and quite often your subjects will be prepared to forego part of their break to help you in your experiment. Although the author has often found subjects to be very accommodating on this matter, it is not something that can be counted on, and certainly not something that can be abused. It is necessary for your own planning and administration purposes to find out when the breaks are as soon as possible, and fit them into your procedure. There is also a better than evens chance that you will also want a break yourself before the experiment is far gone.

Be warned also that there are a large number of people around – men and women – whose lunch will regularly consist of a few pints of beer, gin and tonics or similar beverage. Is your experiment sensitive to alcohol? If so, how do you propose to resolve this problem? Friday lunchtimes can be particularly problematical.

Lunch breaks can also introduce other extraneous variables. One experimenter, as part of his study, had to record lung capacity and the force of expulsion of breath from engineering workers. Half-a-dozen of the management took the experimenter out to lunch where they all dined well at a local restaurant on king prawns in garlic. On their return, all the management team underwent his tests. Thereafter, all the workmen complained (quite vociferously) about the odour of garlic coming from the spirometer.

It is worth noting in passing that many laboratory experiments are so refined that they are unable to cope with the invasion of extraneous variables such as those described above. Can you design your *field* experiment with sufficient robustness to accommodate such naturally occurring, if unwanted, variables without compromising the integrity of your experiment?

Summary of section 13

1 An experiment is not only *run*, it has to be administered. Administration needs to be planned for if it is to be implemented smoothly.
2 A key implement in successful administration is the establishment of an experimental or psychologial 'ops room'. This is frequently a room in the target building, but could easily be a trailer, van, portakabin, or even a tent.
3 Rest periods and breaks from work possess an importance to your subjects which can be easily overlooked. Take them into account, plan for them and build in your own breaks. On no account should you set up your experimental ops room in a canteen or works rest room.
4 Many laboratory experiments are so refined that they are unable to cope with an influx of extraneous variables. The field experiment must be sufficiently robust that it can accommodate such variables without compromising either its sensitivity or integrity.

14   Administration versus Experimentation

A field experiment can come to grief for one of many reasons. Many of the causes of failure in the preparation and planning phase were discussed in section 4. It is, however, still possible for an experiment to fail during the field phase. Without doubt the most frequent cause of such failure, particularly common to students new to field work, is their insistence on trying to run both the experiment and the administration by themselves. In very few cases will the psychologist be able to do both without conflict arising somewhere in the experiment. In field work, at least one other person will be required to help the experimenter with the nitty-gritty aspects of running the experimental trials. This is where assistants come into their own. They also come in various forms. They can be colleagues, fellow students, spouses, and so on. In the case of student projects it is worthwhile doubling-up with a fellow student(s) so that each can assist at the other's trials.

You may also find that the host organization will allocate someone to help you in your experiments. They may not be with you for the whole duration of the trials but they can often be useful in the initial phase in helping to set up equipment and in obtaining subjects. Those people who have been allocated to help you will often be young apprentices, junior secretaries or sometimes members of middle-management or their equivalent in whichever organization you have selected. If your trials are to take place over one day or less then the chances are that these people will be allocated to you for the duration, otherwise they may be released to you for set periods only, or they may be available 'on call'. Such people can be a great help to the experimenter not least because they tend to know where most things are in the organization and who to contact for any specialist help. However, you must be aware of the problems of confidentiality (see section 17.3 on real subjects and section 24 on ethical factors in behavioural research).

There is little doubt that one of the best people in an organization to have on your side is the site or company nurse. Nurses may be employed by an organization on either a full- or part-time basis depending usually on the size of the organization and the nature (hazardous or otherwise) of the work the company is engaged in. Nurses tend to be interested in matters psychological and are often happy to support you in your studies providing that they themselves are not too busy and the requests made of them by the experimenter are reasonable. Their knowledge of the organization they work for and their position in it are invaluable. Also as nurses they are used to, and can be trusted with, confidential information. Finally, if your research has implications for health and safety at work, then it is courteous to inform the company nurse and/or doctor of your plans.

Your assistants, whether colleagues, fellow students or whomever must be used wisely. They do not need to have an in-depth knowledge of your particular research area but they do need to know what you want them to do. Do not just tell your assistants what you want, *show* them; give them an actual demonstration of your experiment and, if possible, take them by the metaphorical hand and walk them through a practise run. If they cannot run the study without your physically being there and watching over them then you have not briefed them properly. You will also gain by this because there is nothing like explaining yourself to others for clarifying your own mind.

Summary of section 14

1 The most common cause of an experiment coming to grief in the field is the assumption by the experimenter that he or she can handle both the experimentation and the administration simultaneously. Rarely is this possible, and any attempt to do so will soon produce conflict.
2 If you are to successfully carry off an applied experiment under field conditions you will need assistance. Support may come from within, such as colleagues or fellow students, or without, such as company personnel.
3 Any assistant must be well briefed and used wisely. They must never be misused or taken for granted.

15   Primed Experiments

It is the usual practice for experimenters to run their own experiments. That is, they have command and control over every aspect of the experiment as it evolves. Some experiments however cannot be administered by the experimenter in such a straightforward and desirable manner. Operationally they have to be run at arm's length. These 'one-removed' types of experiment the author generally refers to as *primed* experiments, because the experimenter has to set up the experiment (or prime it) and then stand back and let it run its course. These experiments are characterized by the fact that at some time in the administration of your experiment you are forced to let go. This is not an easy thing to do.

It is always assumed in lectures and text books that the experimenter will be on-site (or in the laboratory) to run his or her experiment at first hand, with or without an assistant. There are some occasions however when this is simply not possible, often for operational reasons. The most common situation is where the experiment is being conducted in a physical or operational environment in which the experimenter cannot venture. A classic example of a primed experiment is one which is carried out in space. In the Soviet space station *Mir* or the US space shuttle *Challenger*, scientific experiments are carried out routinely by cosmonauts and astronauts who are not the originators of the experiments. Other examples include experiments run inside aircraft cockpits, down mines, in military areas and in sundry environments such as the jungle, desert, Arctic, underwater and outer space. The author has previously mentioned one student who primed one of her experiments to be run by an army unit in a location which was particularly hot and humid. The nature of the study dictated that it would be impossible for her to be present during the trials so she primed her experiment to run without her being on-site. Such procedures are not to be used lightly as being divorced both physically and administratively from a study can produce a discomforting level of anxiety within the isolated experimenter.

One reason for running a primed experiment is that the study can be 'piggy-backed' onto another activity. For example, you may be interested in cognitive performance during adaptation to high temperatures, and are particularly keen to run a field experiment under natural conditions. You discover that an oil company is about to send a team of geologists and technicians to the western desert in Australia, and you ask if the team could carry out some trials for you. Naturally, your study must not interfere with their own field work so you piggy back your experiment onto the oil company's project. Piggy backing experiments can be an effective way of conducting field projects but it requires a high degree of empathy with both your host and your subjects.

A primed experiment seems to possess some rather attractive points, not least being the fact that once the experiment is under way, the experimenter can sit back and wait for the data to roll in. To take full advantage of this situation the experimenter must possess a natural element of imperturbability. Its main advantage, however, is that a scientific study can be run in an environment which would normally be denied to the experimenter.

The essence of a primed experiment is that someone other than the experimenter administers the experimental trials. This stand-in may be an intermediary such as a supervisor or team leader, or they may even be one or more of your subjects. Consequently, in a primed experiment, the administrative details must be explained clearly and thoroughly. You will rarely be able to intervene, even verbally, once the study is under way. The instructions should be confined to those points relevant to the administration of the experimental trials. These instructions should also be given in writing in the form of an *aide-mémoire*. A modified copy of the functional specification can prove very useful here. Make it a point in primed experiments to conduct *rehearsals* of the experimental procedures with your stand-ins. In some designs you will run controlled trials prior to the experimental trials and these are excellent rehearsal sessions.

It is important to ensure that all the data which are collected during these trials can be safely stored and passed on to you as smoothly and securely as possible. Also, thought must be given to the future of the test apparatus once the data have been collected. Can it be recovered immediately upon completion of the tests? Will it have to remain in the field until the primary activities of your subjects have been completed? If the latter is the case, you should consider whether 'drop off' and 'pick up' points can be arranged (they usually can); after all, your subjects will not thank you if they have to continue carrying experimental apparatus around with them wherever they go. These points are emphasized because there is a tendency to believe that once the data have been collected the experiment as far as the subject is concerned is effectively finished. This is not always so, and certainly not the case in a primed experiment. Consequently, it is essential for the experimenter to think the whole experiment through *from the subject's point of view*.

Yet another reason for choosing a primed experiment is to circumvent the lack of resources which currently bedevils scientific research. Furthermore, it may not be possible to spend three months in the field with a group of subjects to collect, say, six hours' worth of data. Running experiments in tropical climes might seem attractive but the funding is rarely there to see it through at first hand. Again, the experimenter may be debarred from certain environments because of the lack of training or expertise; for example, all personnel who work offshore must hold in-date sea survival and lifeboat handling certificates. It may not be possible for the experimenter to acquire these due to a lack of time, money or both – or even because of the strong demand for the survival training courses by regular offshore workers. In other fields, the experimenter may be denied access for reasons of insurance or health and safety.

As one would expect there are disadvantages to primed experiments. The obvious one is that at some stage the trials are beyond the influence of the experimenter. This can cause problems with features of administration which may need routine adjusting to keep the experiment on course. The main problem is that unexpected extraneous variables can arise which influence the outcome of the experiment, but which will go unobserved by the experimenter. The stand-ins tasked with administering the experiment on your behalf may not report extraneous variables because they either did not notice them, or they thought them unimportant, or they were so obvious that the experimenter must be aware of them anyway! It is guaranteed that everyone else will have different assumptions concerning your experiment than you yourself have.

In conclusion, a *primed* experiment differs operationally from a normal experiment to a degree sufficient to warrant separate consideration. Primed experiments have both advantages and disadvantages over the more normal type of experiment and should be used with caution.

SAQ 12
When can you legitimately use a primed experiment?

Summary of section 15

1 There are certain types of field experiment from which the experimenter may be physically barred at certain times. This could be for operational reasons, or for reasons of health and safety, administration, or even through a simple lack of resources.
2 In order to run the trials at all the experimenter must prime the experiment in such a way that effective results can still be obtained without the experimenter being present and *without* compromising the integrity of the experimental design.
3 The main advantage of a primed experiment is that the researcher can still obtain valid data, albeit at one remove.
4 The main disadvantage is that the researcher must relinquish direct control over the experiment at some stage, which means that procedurally corrective action may not be taken, and unexpected extraneous variables may be missed altogether.
5 Only prime an experiment if there really is no other way. A primed experiment is a last resort.

16   Record-keeping and Documentation

In a laboratory experiment it is essential to maintain adequate records of your research. In a field experiment this is critical for, unlike a laboratory experiment, there is rarely an opportunity for going back. Many students approach record-keeping with a sinking feeling and usually limit themselves to writing down the scores or data as they appear. This is woefully inadequate and it is not uncommon for student projects to come unstuck for want of supporting documentation. Conversely, the ability to refer to adequate records after the event can often save the day. Below are described two items, the *experimental diary* and the *site diary*, which are essential to the adequate recording of field experiments. A few other items which may prove useful are described at the end.

Before considering the documents themselves a few words are in order about the very task of writing up diaries or log books. Firstly, keeping a diary is a disciplined activity. This act will itself introduce a discipline into your project, and have a direct and beneficial effect on the planning. Secondly, diaries are a means of logging experience. This is a very important function, because you will soon find that in the real world formal methods and skills will go only so far. If you wish to venture successfully beyond that you will need to fall back on experience. Thirdly, many people who keep working or project diaries report a direct link between writing and action. Diary entries are usually made at the time of the event (as with a log book). Later they will support an active reflection of the situation, and a reflection moreover which is a continual process. This reflection, in turn, enhances the understanding of the problems and options available and helps to clarify the different, and often conflicting, situations which arise. Fourthly, as well as enabling the researcher to reflect upon the experiment or project itself, a well-kept diary also encourages reflection upon experimental and work practices. It has been reported that work diaries have helped to establish and refine new working habits and practices.

Now, when it comes to keeping and writing up your own site diary or log book, there is no set way, no hard-and-fast rule on how to best go about it. At first you will need to experiment with different styles until one is developed which fulfils well the function of a log and which is also comfortable and easy to maintain. This will become your own style. Do avoid the superficial. Do not bother about making rough drafts before entering it into your log. This takes up too much time and encourages rough writing. Enter your notes straight into the log and practise will ensure that the entries are neat, legible and sensible.

Many people consider diaries to be very personal documents and, of course, personal diaries are. But work diaries are not personal items, they log project experience which is transferable to other projects and other people. A log book is a means of communication and to this end it must be available to others in your team. In large research programmes, or even student projects where more than one experimenter (or experimenter plus assistants) are involved then it is worth keeping a *collective* diary. Collective diaries are true log books and are a tremendous asset in communicating between team members. They are also extremely effective in helping to establish working practices and procedures, whether they be experimental, operational or administrative.

Finally, do remember that a diary or log book is a necessary functional tool. You are not writing a novel.

16.1   *Experimental diary*

The experimental diary should contain the running details of the actual experiment. All experimental results and data should be logged and it is advisable to draw up blank tables before the experiment into which the data can be inserted. The experimental diary is begun long before the field experiment is run. It will contain written details of the experimental design and procedure, proposed analyses, important references, checklists of experimental and support equipment, etc. During the experiment, as well as logging data, you should also record any modifications which you have had to make in the design or procedure which may have arisen by, for example, your subjects not being available in the order you had wanted, having to make a last minute change in the site location, being forced by circumstances to run your tests in a different order than the one you had originally planned, and so on. If some of your data are recorded in graphical form (e.g. ECG readings) or are logged directly into the microcomputer, a practice which is becoming more common these days, then a 'hard copy' printout of the data should be taken and included in the experimental diary.

The form the experimental diary takes depends on the personal preference of the experimenter, but one of the most useful is a simple A4 size ring binder. This allows various types of documentation, charts, photographs, tables, etc. to be easily included and arranged in the diary. Although, the A4 size binder has its advantages there are occasions when the smaller A5 size of ring binder can be more useful because it is easier to pack and transport.

16.2   Site diary

You *must* keep a site diary. This is very important. You will be surprised at the number of times that you will have cause to refer to this diary, both during and especially after your experimental trials. Many students initially question the burden of taking on more paperwork, but once persuaded to keep such a diary, they have subsequently found it to be worth its weight in gold.

The site diary can be considered as analogous to a ship's log and in it you record the main non-scientific events which occur during the project, as well as all deviations, abnormalities and administrative details. These can include all relevant telephone calls as well as the results of any meetings between yourself and your supervisor, the host organization and any others as well as more formal details such as your time of arrival on site, the person you should report to, where and when, the time your trials commenced, the time at which the mobile ECG or tachistoscope jammed, what went wrong with it, the time at which it was fixed and back on-line, who fixed it, and so on. Also you must include the names of the people you met and worked with on-site in the course of your study, along with their relevant details, for example, managing director, chief storeman, course instructor, supervisor, investment analyst, staff nurse, plus their telephone number or other point of contact. It is important to record information concerning any equipment or facilities belonging to the host organization which are used or borrowed by you, along with details of when you borrowed them, from whom and when they were returned. It is not uncommon to receive telephone calls asking if you are still in possession of a certain item of equipment which you returned previously, as the company cannot find it. If you have kept full records of the event, then it is a simple matter to resolve the situation; if you have not, then you can be in for some awkwardness.

As well as being an important organizational record, site diaries also serve another purpose: they make fine personal records of the joys and frustrations of conducting individual research in the field. They also serve as an excellent *aide-mémoire* for when you are planning further field studies, as well as helping to smooth the way for others who are just beginning to conduct applied psychological experiments. You can be sure that the very mistakes which you first logged in your site diary, and which now with hindsight seem so naïve and obvious, are still being made by others today. It is the site diary, not the experimental diary, in which your hard-won experience is encapsulated.

The most appropriate document for a site diary is a bound A5 sized notebook with stiff covers and a goodly number of pages. The use of a loose-leaf folder is advised against as these are not sufficiently permanent. Unlike experimental diaries, where data and information are being constantly transferred in and out, the site diary is a more permanent record. Choose one with margins down both sides of the page, or alternatively draw your own margins. The body of the page is used to log the key events, while the margins are reserved for jotting down those ideas which will crop up continuously throughout the project.

Do bear in mind the bottom line; that is, in applied work circumstances can change, through no fault of your own, which can cause your project to crash. In this event your site diary is your insurance. A meticulously maintained site diary will still provide something substantial to show your supervisor or examining board. It really is worth the premium.

On the more optimistic side, well maintained site and experimental diaries mean that your final report is already half written.

SAQ 13
Why do you need two diaries?

16.3   *Memorandum*

A memo book can be a very useful item or it can be redundant. The choice is yours and depends very much on the type and the form of your experiment. If you are running a team project or conducting experimental trials over a number of periods which possibly involves more than one site or department, then you may well find yourself sending hand-written messages or memoranda to various bodies in order to assist you in coordinating the experiment. If you do find yourself in this position, then you are strongly advised to record all your messages in a thick, soft-covered memo pad, which has a carbon copy facility and numbered pages. With this type of memo pad all your messages and notices which are sent, are automatically recorded in a single bound permanent volume for future reference.

16.4   Progress reports

If the research study is one which will run over several weeks or possibly months then the student should submit regular progress reports. These reports are important. They provide feedback to the student, the supervisor and the host organization (if necessary) on the current status and progress of the project. The information contained in these reports serve to identify the current problems and future errors which may then be corrected or interdicted.

Progress reports should be structured. They should be prepared on forms which are simple in design and the information reported must be organized and regular. Essay-style reports are *not* what is wanted. All reports should relate directly to the project plan, and only information pertaining to the progress of the project should be included, i.e. advances made in relation to the planned timetable, activities completed, goals/milestones achieved and any technical difficulties encountered.

How frequently should progress reports be submitted? Quite simply, as often as necessary. For a substantial project (undergraduate or postgraduate) then once a month is usually optimum. Any longer and the risk is increased of the project drifting off course unnoticed, any shorter and reporting becomes a chore with redundancy or duplication creeping into the information. With shorter projects it may be more appropriate to submit reports once a fortnight.

Progress reports are a key tool in project control. The chief beneficiary is the researcher.

16.5   Miscellaneous

You may need to keep further records and documentation in addition to those described above, depending very much on the type of experiments you are carrying out and where they are being run. For example, at the most basic level copies of all correspondence associated with the experiments should be kept in a separate file. At a more involved level you may find yourself running some experimental studies at the request of a particular organization (i.e. contract research). If this is so then you must have drawn up and agreed, before you begin your studies, a set procedure for incorporating changes after the study has commenced. If you are conducting a programme of research on behalf of an organization or company, it is not uncommon to find that your hosts or client will want to make alterations to the study when it is but part-way through. This situation should be resisted as much as possible, not least because of the difficulty in obtaining data retrospectively. Such circumstances usually arise for one of three reasons: firstly, the hosts were not quite sure what research they wanted done in the first place. In other words they did not have a clear idea of the problem. This situation is extremely common. Secondly, they have just thought of something else which they believe to be relevant to the study and they now think it ought to be included. Thirdly, and rather sadly, there are people around who will already have made up their minds what the answers are to be and your studies serve merely to confirm their views. If your findings differ from these views they may either ignore your work or will endeavour to alter your study in some appreciable way so that the findings do finally reflect what they wish them to. The first two points are quite common in contract research, the third is comparatively rare but still exists, and the author has had personal experience of all three at work. Contract research is a separate topic in its own right and beyond the scope of this book.

Summary of section 16

1 Systematic and thorough records are essential for the success of any applied study. Experimental and site diaries are key parts of project records.
2 Diary-keeping is a disciplined activity which when mastered will show itself to much advantage in project planning and management.
3 Diary-writing is a form of active reflection which enhances understanding of the project and helps to resolve the many conflicting situations which arise. It also assists in the formation and refinement of new working practices.
4 You must develop your own style of diary-writing.
5 Collective diaries are useful in large projects.
6 At least two diaries or log books are essential:
  (a) *Experimental diary*. This contains the running details of the experiment including results and data.
  (b) *Site diary*. This is equivalent to a ship's log and contains the operational, field and administrative details of the project.
7 Progress reports are a key tool in project control. They should be simply designed but informative and submitted regularly.

17   Subjects

For the most part, the general public (non-psychologists that is) are happy to take part in psychology experiments. This is usually one of the first surprises which greets an experimenter who is more often used to the difficulties of trying to raise enthusiasm among his or her fellow students for such projects. Indeed, so willing to take part are members of the general public, that they may feel hurt if they are not included in your study. One team of stockbrokers the author used as subjects actually split into two social groups – those who had been tested and those who had not. They treated it almost as a 'rite of passage'. This willingness to take part in your project often stems from one or more of the following factors: firstly, people are generally interested in anything which concerns themselves; secondly, your attention to them during the experiment will tend to make them feel important; thirdly, you have novelty value.

As people are the grist to your experimental mill it is worth considering them in a bit more detail.

17.1   Informing your subjects

Your subjects will generally like to know what you are doing and why you are doing it. A few will actually insist on knowing. This is not surprising as, after all, their involvement in your experiment is to them a very personal matter. You will occasionally come across the odd person or two who does not want to know what your experiment is about, and cares even less. This is not to say that they are not willing to take part in your study, but that they will demonstrate this willingness by simply turning up, doing what is required of them then leaving. All with hardly a word spoken. A brief word about the other extreme is also in order here: one day, if you decide to stay in field work, you will come across a small percentage of your subjects who, although naïve to experimental methods, procedures and analysis, will nonetheless sit down and proceed to tell you quite calmly what is wrong with your experiment and why, in their opinion, it will not work. If, as is often the case, they do not know what they are talking about, then patiently hear them through and then try to persuade them to take part in your experiment even with all its faults. If, on the other hand, their criticisms are valid (and remember your subjects may have knowledge of *operational* reasons unknown to you as to why your experiment will not work) then get this person on your side and pump him or her for all they are worth.

Try to inform your potential subjects about the purpose of your experiment as early as possible. One of the best times for doing this is during the site reconnaissance (see section 8 on site reconnaissance). It is usually not difficult to arrange to speak to your subjects in a group, even on open work sites, during one of your pre-trial visits to the organization. You will have to arrange this for yourself because it is unlikely that anyone in the host organization would have thought that you might need to speak to your subjects beforehand. Your presentation should be short and general. The minimum information your subjects will require includes:

- Who you are
- Where you are from
- What you are doing
- Why you are doing it
- What, in very general terms, you want your audience to do for you
- What, if anything, is in it for them (very important!).

Your presentation should be prepared well in advance and it should be prepared thoroughly. Do not be slick, as this will put people on the defensive. The success of your experiment will depend on whether or not you can get your potential subjects behind you. You cannot order them to take part – you must convince them.

Unless you are planning to use as your subjects the board of directors of a particular organization, or perhaps the Chief of the Defence Staff, then the chances are that the people you will want to use will themselves have superiors within the workplace. These people will usually take the form of 'management'. When presenting a case and asking for volunteers from a group to take part in an experiment, the author always likes to speak to the group without the presence in the room of management, officers, supervisors, instructors or whomever. This is particularly important in cases where you are dealing with more or less captive groups such as members of the armed forces, offshore workers, etc. You should also be aware of peer pressure and build in an escape route for your subjects. In simple terms, do not ask for a show of hands for volunteers.

SAQ 14
Why should you not ask for volunteers?

You must have the means of allowing your subjects to come to you confidentially and say that they do not wish to take part in your experiment, and they should be fully aware of the fact that they can do this. Should anyone approach you and say they do not wish to take part then you have *no* right to an explanation or reason from them. Say quite simply that their withdrawal is perfectly okay, that their decision to withdraw remains between you and them and thank them for giving you their time so far. Having said this you will be pleasantly surprised to find that very few people indeed will want to withdraw from your experiment although this will, of course, depend on the nature of the experiment. Of those who do refuse to take part, see below.

A simple way of preparing the ground for your study is to put a notice on the various noticeboards throughout the organization. The note should be written in general and concise terms and, ideally, be typed onto your departmental headed paper. The person in the host organization with whom you are liaising may agree to pass on information sheets to your subjects. This can be a very effective method *if it works*. Unfortunately, it happens too many times that the subjects have not received the explanation forms by the time you arrive to begin the trials. You will find that this is still the case even when you have dispatched the forms weeks before you need to start testing. Alternatively, you can write to your subjects individually, although some people will view the brown envelopes with suspicion. Nonetheless, a set of pre-experiment briefing notes sent to each subject is the best way to inform. If you are sending these notes through the host organization, then you need to confirm near the time of your trials that they have actually got through to your subjects and are not piled up in a pending tray somewhere. This situation arises too often and you find your subjects turning up on the day of the experiment claiming rightly that this is the first that they have heard of it and what is it all about? This is one situation which you cannot allow to happen. If you have any doubts about the *content* of your message getting across to your subjects then discuss it with one of the more senior members of the group, for example, the foreman or a supervisor or a section head and ask for his or her advice. They will know their people better than you ever will, and will often feel flattered at being asked in the first place.

At some stage you will undoubtedly tap into the organization's 'grapevine'. At times this can be a good thing and you will end up with subjects forming long queues outside your cubby-hole, banging on the door demanding to be experimented on. On the other hand it can trigger lots of trouble. On one occasion the author was conducting some psychological tests on a group of engineers who, quite coincidentally, just happened at that time to be working on a sealed-off chemically contaminated area. The fact that the work-site was contaminated had absolutely no bearing on the experiment. Because certain physiological data was also required, and to ease administration, permission was obtained to run the psychological tests at the same time as the engineers were undergoing their standard annual health-and-safety medical examination. Word soon telegraphed down the grapevine, particularly amongst those people on the site who were not involved in the experiment, that this year's medical was different and involved more people than usual. Rumours spawned and spread and shortly after lunchtime we discovered, to our consternation, that certain representatives of the media had appeared at the main security gate wanting to know why '. . . the place was crawling with psychiatrists?'. In this particular instance the psychological experiments we were running were private experiments and in no way connected with the function of the organization. Fortunately, once the situation had been diffused, the management found the whole thing quite amusing. There was a moment, however, when goodwill was strained. Be warned also that there are some people around who will be out to deliberately misinterpret your intentions. There will not be many, but it only takes one. Brief your host organization and your subjects well and rumours will be still-born.

Summary of section 17.1

1 You must at all times keep your subjects informed of what you are about. Brief them early and keep them updated. This is the least you owe your subjects.
2 Brief your subjects on:
   - *Who* you are
   - *Where* you are from
   - *What* you are doing
   - *Why* you are doing it
   - *What* you want them to do
   - *What* is in it for them.
3 You must allow each subject a means of withdrawing from your study without producing either conflict with their superiors or loss of face with their peers. Peer pressure can be very powerful in some groups.
4 Do not be afraid to ask the group leader for help or advice in briefing your subjects.
5 Be aware of the organization's grapevine. They all have one. Ensure that all unwanted rumours are still-born by keeping your subjects and the host organization thoroughly informed at all times.

17.2   Subject resistance

The topic of subject resistance has been touched on previously and this phenomenon will now be considered in some more detail as it can be very important.

Consider the following situation: you are well under way with your experiment, all is going well, the data are coming in smoothly, and then one of your subjects blatantly refuses to take part. This situation is not very common, indeed the author has in the past tested what must be bordering on several hundred people within their respective natural environments, and put the number of those who refused to take part at under 20. A subject refusal may come as a surprise for two reasons: firstly, because such a rejection is inconsistent with the attitude and approach of the rest of your subject group and secondly, because the response given may be more hostile than such a situation really warrants. There are usually two reasons for such a reaction. The first is quite understandable, and has possibly happened to you already, while the second tends to be a bit more sinister. The first reason for such a refusal is that the person concerned is quite simply having a hard day. He or she has perhaps just returned from a meeting out of which they did badly, perhaps their equipment, computer or tools have broken down or they may have been caught in a traffic jam coming into work or perhaps they have personal problems or difficulties at home. They may decide quite simply to get back at life by having a go at you. After all, what can you do? You will often be perceived as being some formless 'establishment' figure, but you will possess no official authority. In these instances the subject will usually come straight out and say to you, 'I'm not interested' or, 'I don't want to play' or some similar straightforward expression. What do you do? You should just shrug your shoulders, say 'fair enough', and go and grab your next subject. There is, after all, nothing you really can do. Quite often the person concerned will come up to you later and say that they have changed their mind and are prepared to take part after all.

The second most common reason for a subject refusal is not quite so easy to resolve. Sometimes people have things to hide. Not unnaturally they tend to be rather frightened of their secret being discovered, usually because it will affect their jobs. Their apprehension is often based on the fact that the public, rightly or wrongly, endow psychologists with an uncanny ability to uncover their innermost secrets. So, what sort of personal secrets can be uncovered and are they really *that* serious? Here are three examples that have come to light while running psychological experiments in the field.

On one occasion it was discovered that one of the managers, who claimed a vocational qualification from a foreign university which was necessary for the job he held, was not in fact so qualified. It turned out that his degree certificates were forged. To compound the matter the membership he had obtained, partly on the basis of these qualifications, from a British chartered institute was consequently invalid. This person had been working for the same firm for a number of years and was regarded as being very good at his job.

On another occasion a middle-grade manager in his early forties was found to have a history of alcohol abuse which he was hiding from his employers and his friends. This person was very frightened that his addiction to alcohol, if discovered, would result in his losing his job. No one else in the organization appeared to be aware of his personal situation.

Although not personally involved in the third example, the author was reliably informed by another experimenter that he discovered the same subject turning up at two different work-sites but under different names and even with different national insurance numbers! Such practices are not uncommon in certain quarters.

People who are worried that you may, in the course of your experiment, uncover something that they do not want known will rarely say outright that they are not interested in taking part. Rather they will tend to offer excuses for not being able to do your tests. For example, being too busy to take part is an easy one to fall back on. It is true that there are times when people are too busy, but they will usually be happy to suggest a time which is more convenient to them. The subject who is refusing never will. They may also try to rationalize the situation away; for example they may say, 'Oh I don't believe in this sort of thing' as though you were trying to entice them into some magical rite.

What do you do in such situations? There is no easy answer to this question and each case must be treated on its own merits. On no account should you breach confidence and on no account become directly involved yourself. If you believe that you have stumbled across something which genuinely requires attention then seek specialist guidance. One useful source is the medical practitioner and the nurse. These people are professionals who deal daily in confidential and personal problems and have their own private channels of communication. Only accept a source who can truly help and assist the subject, not one who can but judge and condemn.

Occasionally you will come across what can be considered as modified acceptance to your request for volunteers. It has happened, for example, that a young woman will only agree to being tested if her 'best friend' can come along too. Depending on the nature of your experiment this may be a bit of a nuisance, however in most cases it is usually possible to meet such requests. Even if meeting such a request will increase the overhead in your resources. It is often best to go along with the subject's wishes where practical in order to maintain the goodwill of the rest of the group.

Occasionally, the whole group of subjects may refuse *en masse* to take part in your study. If this happens then look for two things: firstly, an underlying conflict involving organizational politics and secondly, a ring-leader. More is said on the matter of organizational politics in section 25. Another explanation for mass refusal, of course, is that the problem lies with *you*! You may simply have failed to win the trust or commitment of your subjects.

Summary of section 17.2

1 Subject resistance to taking part in an experiment is not very common in the real world. When it does arise it may do so for one of two reasons:
   (i)   The person has just had a hard day at work or at home or both. If their problems are temporary then so will be their resistance.
   (ii) The person has something to hide. This situation must be approached with care and common sense.
2 If your subjects refuse *en masse* to take part then this is frequently due to:
   (i)   Underlying organizational politics.
   (ii) Your failure to win their trust and commitment.

17.3   Real subjects

When you go out into the field to conduct your first experiment you will meet people of all shapes, sizes, creeds, colours and temperaments. *All these people have but one purpose in this life. That purpose is to foul-up your experiment.* For the most part they will not do it deliberately; indeed, few will realize that by some innocent action they have just demolished an experimental design of outstanding beauty and refinement. Moreover, the ability to reduce experimental psychologists to the foetal position, which these people possess, appears to be innate and some are really quite gifted. Some phrases frequently to be heard on the lips of your subjects will include: 'Is this yours, it came off in my hand?'; 'But when your mate said stand on the *test* piece, I thought he meant *that*' (pointing to a tachistoscope/ECG/tape recorder, etc.); 'I can't do these tests – you see, I can't read'. All these, and many similar types of incident, have actually happened. There was also the occasion when one of the author's groups of subjects failed to complete all the phases of an experiment because they went out on the town one night and were arrested.

These discomforts to the experimenter can be frustrating but they are usually innocent. Occasionally, however, one or two of your subjects may seek to disrupt your study deliberately or to cause some particular embarrassment to the experimenter. This is rarely done with any malice aforethought but usually because, '. . . it's a bit of a laugh for the lads, eh?'. Their intention is quite simply to have a harmless laugh at your expense. They are, of course, completely unaware that this may destroy your experiment. On arrival at Aberdeen, a team of returning off-shore oil rig workers were interviewed for a final-year student project by two young female sociology students. As their sociological questions became more involved and personal the oil rig workers began to take great pleasure in convincing these, perhaps surprisingly naïve, youngsters that they, the riggers, all managed to cope successfully with long periods of confinement at sea because they were all of homosexual inclination. They all agreed that this led to a quiet life off-shore except on wash days. Be warned and be on your guard.

Groups of men with a high spirit of camaraderie are particularly prone to this sort of caper, e.g. members of the armed forces, commercial divers, miners, welders, truck drivers, police officers, etc. One female experimenter, a civilian, went to carry out some psychological tests on a group of soldiers. The soldiers had been briefed prior to the day of the experiment on what was required and had been ordered to report to a room for testing as a group. When the experimenter arrived she found the soldiers sitting round a table wearing standard army uniform and balaclavas and resolutely refusing to give their name, rank or number on the grounds of 'security'. It was the first time the experimenter had been involved in this sort of field work and for a while she was at a loss at what to do. The situation was brought quickly to a halt by the colonel who happened to be walking by the office and saw what was happening. During a completely different study, on an all-male engineering work site, one subject turned up for testing wearing a safety hat, safety boots and nothing else. When asked why he had turned up in such a manner the subject replied, 'Well, it's the health and safety at work act'. In this instance the male experimenter had worked on this particular site in the past and had been warned that something like this would be inflicted on him by this particular character. The experimenter's solution to the problem was to continue with the test as though nothing had happened, having previously opened the windows and closed down the central heating in the portakabin which served as his testing room. The testing took a good half hour to complete and it was winter. The subject's workmates thoroughly enjoyed the way the tables had been turned and became more than willing to help out on any further experiments.

One thing to be very wary of amongst such subjects is the confidentiality of test results. In many instances you will be testing some aspect of a subject's performance. People who work in the same group are interested not only in their own performance but also in how it relates to other members of the group. In these cases it is quite common for subjects to ask, not only for their own particular test scores, but also for the scores of their friends and workmates. A close-knit group sees nothing wrong in this. Whether or not you release to your subjects their own scores will usually depend on the nature of the experiment. *On no account whatsoever* are you to divulge the scores, no matter how apparently harmless, of the person's workmates. When you refuse to release these scores the subject may persist on another tack. For example, he may say, 'Okay, but can you tell me just if I did better or worse than Joe on this particular test'.

He will also insist that he and Joe are the best of buddies and have been friends ever since childhood, and anyway Joe would not mind. Again, the response from you is a firm but polite 'no'. It will usually suffice to explain that you are bound by the same laws of ethics and confidentiality as, say, a priest or a doctor. The fact that at the end of the day when you call into the local for a drink and there you find all your subjects publicly deriding each other's test scores (which you went to great pains to issue individually and confidentially) should make no difference to your approach on this matter. On a more practical note you may well hear that Joe, who is not your subject's best friend after all, is combing the worksite with a monkey-wrench looking for you.

You should also expect to have words put into your mouth. Walking past a mess room after a testing session a researcher overheard the passing comment, 'Hey Bill, it's official, you *really* are thick – the doctor said so!'. Unfortunately, the battle between experimenter and subjects is rarely evenly matched. Nature herself has been known to join the fray against the researcher as have other, supposedly non-participating, persons. Dr Duncan Godden (1975) reports some of the problems he faced using divers as subjects on the River Cam while trying to run an experiment into context-dependent memory underwater:

> Enthusiastic punters had to be restrained from spiking divers with their poles, while a group of academic-looking nudists lurked in the bushes, supposedly fulfilling an old Cambridge tradition.

Finally, if it is of any consolation, our laboratory-based colleagues also face difficulties with their subjects. In an experiment carried out in 1963 at Harvard University into reasoning behaviour and the generation of rules to eliminate hypotheses, the subjects were asked if their rule was incorrect, how could they find out? The experimenters report (Wason and Johnson-Laird, 1968):

> Nine subjects replied that they would continue to generate series consistent with their hypothesis and wait for one to be negative; two replied that they would try out other hypotheses (the rational answer); three replied that no other rules were possible. . . . One subject did not make any announcement. Unfortunately, he developed psychotic symptoms in the middle of the experiment and had to be removed by ambulance.

Summary of section 17.3

1 Be aware of your subjects at all times. In the real world they have an uncanny ability to destroy experiments quite innocently.
2 A few subjects may set out to test the experimenter. This will not be

done with any malice, but merely to raise a laugh for their group. You will not survive long in the real world without a sense of humour.

3 In any battle between subjects and experimenter you can guarantee that Nature will side with your subjects.

4 *All test results are confidential.* On no account must results be released to anyone except the subject from whom they were obtained.

17.4   Experimenters and what to watch out for

Many students undertaking applied experimental psychology in field settings will often, when going onto a worksite for the very first time, experience some degree of what may best be described as 'sub-culture shock'. It cannot be denied that most students have had a middle-class upbringing and have often come directly from school to university or polytechnic. The groups from which you will draw your experimental subjects will often have different values, attitudes, levels of education, interests, etc. Short of actually living and working with your subjects there is little that can be done to overcome some initial surprise and perhaps discomfort. Being prepared for it can help.

The extent of the difficulty facing certain young students new to field experiments was highlighted one day when a very recently qualified graduate began testing his first batch of fabrication yard workers. He went to great pains to explain to one young worker (about his own age) how to complete an MMPI personality form. After some thought the young lad said he could not do the MMPI. The postgraduate student, with much patience, explained again for a further three times how the form should be completed. Still the subject insisted that he could not do the MMPI. Finally, the experimenter asked why he could not complete the MMPI – 'Because I can't read!', came the reply.

The interesting point here is that the experimenter could not accept that the subject was unable to read and insisted he was just being awkward. There were six people on this site with varying degrees of illiteracy. In this instance the young experimenter, having been brought up to read more or less as a way of life, could not grasp the fact that there are a significant number of people around who are unable to read or write.

Do not be surprised if you also come across people in occupations which appear to be completely out of character. One scraggy-bearded old souser who was dragged away from shovelling mud out of a sump on a building site to take part in an experiment was found, on the initial interview, to have two science degrees and a PhD from Oxbridge under his belt. This was interesting because it had been assumed from the outset that the level of education of labourers on this particular site would be quite low.

It is all too easy, if having been brought up in a comparatively restricted environment, to arrive on a worksite or in a field setting with ideas about your subject sample which are based on preconceived and deeply rooted assumptions. Fortunately, most young experimenters have a fair smattering of common sense and come to understand their new subjects very quickly. Once an understanding, and indeed rapport, has been established between you and your subjects, then research can become very rewarding.

Beware also of becoming isolated from the rest of the host organization, especially if you will be working on site for a long period of time (i.e. in a placement). One student became very depressed during one such placement with a recently privatized major company. Although he said the people he was with were very friendly, they were all engineers and for most of the day he did not understand what they were talking about. Naturally, they knew equally little about psychology. Foolishly, in this instance, instead of tackling the problem head-on (e.g. getting an intelligent layman's command of the subject) he let it wear him down with the result that his work suffered and his project was rescued at the last minute only by a major salvage operation and the initiating of a contingency plan involving people from outside the organization. Any applied experimental psychologist must be able to work comfortably with all sorts of groups and individuals.

Summary of section 17.4

1 A few students will receive a mild shock on entering an outside organization for the first time. Here they meet people with backgrounds, attitudes, education, interests and opinions very different from their own. They also find that they now have to interact with these people with a degree of intimacy which has never been required of them before. Fortunately, most students do have their wits about them and soon come to establish a rapport with their subjects.
2 Beware of becoming isolated within a host organization. You must work comfortably with all sorts of people.

18   Subject Acquisition

In other words, how do you grab people to do your experiment? Rarely will you be allowed to just pull people off their job willy-nilly – even if willy-nilly is the closest you can get to formal sampling (see section 4.4). It is invariably the case that the person you grab will be the only one around who can do that important key job; the one which needs to be done at the very time that you have him or her locked into your experiment. The art of conducting psychological experiments in natural environments is to retain a robust experimental design with *no* disruption to the work of the host organization. This is what you must aim for. To achieve this aim you will need to learn to manage time, facilities and people as effectively as possible, and this includes yourself (see also Part 6 on Project Management Techniques for Field Research).

If all or any part of your experiment can be conducted using groups of subjects, as opposed to individuals, then do so. This can make life much easier for everyone. If your subjects must be tested individually, then arrange for someone in authority to find them for you. It is rare that a group of people needs to be tested in a specific sequence, but if this is the case then draw up a list of the names of your subjects and the order in which you require them and explain why they are needed in such a sequence. You will often find that you will incur a time penalty in such cases and this will need to be planned for.

The job of actually finding people at the right time for your experiment will usually fall to such people as site foremen or engineers, supervisors, deputy managers and such like. Those who hold such positions tend to know both the job and their people and can arrange for the work to continue with the minimum of disruption to either the company or your experiment. Providing the *sequence* of testing is not critical to your design, and the work is flexible, then many subjects appreciate being allowed to arrange their own order for testing. This is to be encouraged whenever it is possible.

Summary of section 18

1 It is rare that you will be able to simply pick subjects for testing when you wish to. You should arrange for someone in authority in the host organization to arrange for your subjects to be released from their jobs at the most appropriate time.
2 It is administratively more effective for subjects to be tested in groups rather than individually and this approach should be aimed for if at all possible.
3 Providing the order in which people are tested is not critical to your design, then allow your subjects to arrange their own testing times and schedules. This is often appreciated.

19   Health and Safety

It is worthwhile briefly mentioning some of the practical aspects of health and safety, if only so you can be forewarned about what to expect. Some experimenters, usually those who are new to field work, fail to appreicate that work sites are potentially dangerous places. They are dangerous even for those who work on them let alone for a visiting researcher. A few minutes' forethought about the practicalities of simply being on your test site can make life much safer and simpler.

There are places which carry minimal regulations and you are able to attend in everyday clothes. These include offices, shops, and many types of factory. Other sites may require you to wear special clothing, such as hard hats, safety glasses, safety boots (i.e. with steel toecaps), overalls, or fluorescent marker jackets, and such like for your own protection. Alternatively, you may be required to wear headgear, overalls, and gloves, for the protection of others, especially if operating in, say, a food-processing unit, or a hospital. If you are operating out of doors, especially in the more exotic environments, then go prepared. One student whose project involved two days and a night in the hills with a university mountaineering club in January, was not fully equipped. This particular researcher spent some uncomfortable time shivering in his tent before the others in the group realized the problem and passed on their spare clothing. This situation is not only extremely dangerous but it does the experiment itself no good at all. It also deals a terrific blow to the experimenter's own credibility.

If in any doubt about the safety requirements of the organization or site where you will be working, then ask. But make sure you ask the right person. Answers such as, 'Oh, it doesn't matter, don't worry about it', do not really help. If specific health and safety regulations are in force at a particular location, you will usually be told about them beforehand. You may even be required to spend some time being briefed by a designated company health and safety officer. One experiment which took place at a refinery required a full morning to be spent in classroom health and safety lectures before being allowed to put a foot on site. Is this time built in to your plan? In many cases, special safety clothing and gear is available on-site to visitors. This is because most sites receive visitors as a matter of course, and safety gear is usually kept in reserve for them. It is, however, the mark of the professional applied experimenter that they turn up with all their own basic safety equipment. Apart from looking after your own safety you will also impress your hosts. For many locations where no specific gear is required a *clean* pair of overalls and suitable footwear are always handy.

You may also need to turn your attention to more personal items, for example, long hair may need to be tied up if operating near machinery, long nails may be impractical in certain circumstances. Hygiene and cleanliness are always important.

Once in your new location check out the emergency exits, fire precautions and so on. Make a note to do this on your checklist because, once on site, you will forget.

This may all seem to be a bit of a chore and health and safety is not the most thrilling part of running a field experiment, but it is important and it may become vital. The wearing of a safety hat can become uncomfortable after a while, but there is a very good reason for doing so. Do not try to buck the system by not wearing a hat just because you are an outsider. After all, the bottom line is always: how much is your head worth to you?

Finally, remember at all times and wherever you are – you are your own safety officer. No-one else is going to look after you.

Summary of section 19

1 Health and safety are important aspects of many applied experimental studies. Many work sites are inherently dangerous places.
2 Ascertain the health and safety policy of the host organization where you are to conduct your experiments and obey it. Do not buck the system.
3 Try to provide your own basic safety gear. It is the stamp of the professional.
4 You are your own safety officer.

In the Field: Dos and Don'ts

Do

- Plan your administration
- Establish an administration room on-site
- Draw up an office/site/layout diagram
- Find out when your subject's breaks are
- Brief your host organization thoroughly
- Brief your host organization well in advance
- Brief your subjects thoroughly

- Brief your assistants thoroughly (show them)
- Check out health and safety regulations
- Try to provide your own basic safety gear
- Keep a site diary
- Provide regular progress reports

Do not

- Neglect administration
- Use canteens or rest rooms as administration or experimental rooms
- Neglect breaks
- Attempt to run both the experiment and the administration by yourself
- Be slick in your briefings
- *Divulge other people's test scores*

Part 4
Back at Base

Sweet analytics, 'tis thou hast ravished me.
Doctor Faustus, CHRISTOPHER MARLOWE (1564–1593)

20   Data Logging and Processing

20.1   Office organization

The key to successful data collection, logging, collation and analysis lies in good office organization. There is no escape from this fact. Good office organization and procedures are important in all research but especially so in field research because of the administrative and practical overheads which are carried by such work. Among other things good organization:

- reduces the workload on the experimenter and his or her assistants;
- reduces unnecessary administrative pressure on the subjects and host organization;
- produces a clear atmosphere in which to work and enables each member of the team to work effectively and efficiently knowing exactly what their responsibilities are.

Although office procedures are mentioned in this section rather than earlier, it goes without saying that careful pre-planning is needed if the most appropriate collection, collation and processing systems are to be selected and an effective routine established. Scientific research can be an exciting and adventurous activity but its backbone is forged from *routine*.

It is true that not everyone, especially students, has access to a formal office. Anyone conducting research, however, must be able to set up an operational base office for the duration of their research project. Ideally, of course, a whole office would be given over to the project, but this is rarely possible even for professional researchers. The 'office' frequently has to be shared with other people and/or other duties not connected with the study. Still, some area must be found and dedicated to the administrative needs of the experiment. This may be only a desk and one wall for chart planners and bulldog clips within the psychology department, or perhaps even a bedroom.

The main point is that whatever is allocated to the experiment as a base office must be reserved solely for that purpose. All data logging, processing and other relevant activities to be carried out in this office must be pre-planned and a system and routine established to support them.

It is important that no activities or material other than those which are relevant to the experiment should be allowed to encroach upon this area. And encroach they will, have no doubt about that. It is a tremendous boost to organization if the chosen area can be marked off physically from all else, even if this can only be achieved by drawing a white line across the floor or marking the area with tape. Mobile screens can help as can rearranged filing cabinets. No matter how it is achieved or how small or large the area, keep it sacrosanct and dedicated to your project. If you cannot keep your own desk clear, then bring in a spare table just for project work.

This base office should be a fixed location, preferably within a psychology department. Mobile offices, such as vehicles or tents are not really suitable because they are too temporary, too cramped and frequently too uncomfortable for prolonged periods of detailed work. They can, however, make an excellent 'ops room' for collecting data in the field and even for initial data analysis. Field ops rooms are described further in section 14.1.

SAQ 15
What are the advantages of good office organization?

20.2   Data processing

Any scientific experiment is an exercise in information processing. The emergence and pervasion of 'information technology' throughout virtually all aspects of our lives today has seeded the concept of information processing as an important activity in its own right.

An experiment is always constructed to capture specific types of data selected to support the *aim* of the experiment. Once captured, the raw data must be processed (analysed) and the results interpreted. With the advancement and ready availability of computerized systems today it is possible to have much experimental data captured at source, stored, analysed and the results displayed for the experimenter in a matter of seconds. This situation is still rare in student projects mostly because of the high level of resources needed to provide the hardware and to write a specific software package to drive the system. This possibility should not be overlooked altogether however, as today all universities, polytechnics and colleges will have young computer buffs around who might be persuaded to write a suitable software package just for the exercise it offers.

Nonetheless, it is still frequently the case that most data are recorded by hand. Personality tests are scored manually, reaction times are jotted into notebooks, verbal responses are recorded on tape recorders and then transcribed, behavioural indicators are observed and noted, errors are counted up and written down, and so on. Under these circumstances, you should ensure that the journey from raw data to polished result is as smooth as possible. It is not uncommon to see students jotting down their experimental data on pieces of torn scrap paper, the backs of envelopes or cigarette packets and even the palms of their hands. This approach to data collection is wholly inadequate as it builds 'risk' into the experiment and encourages sloppy workmanship. These records are never sufficiently permanent or secure, as can be witnessed by the number of students who later report rather sheepishly that they have 'lost' at least some of their data. Furthermore, even if all the data are present it often requires a great deal of back-checking and cross-referencing to sort everything out afterwards. Such methods also reveal, rather blatantly, how the experimenter thinks.

If you have conducted a mock analysis, as suggested in the pilot study stage (see section 6), then you will already have a good idea of how the data should be formatted. Once aware of this format preparing the record forms becomes straightforward. From here data logging is simple. The record forms should be designed and drawn up prior to the experiment. This is well worth the effort even if the form consists of no more than three columns, such as subject number, independent variable measure and dependent variable measure. It is when data on a number of measures have to be obtained that pre-designed, customized record sheets come into their own. Colour coding these sheets is also a great boon to administration. Record sheets are vulnerable to damage and abuse if used out of doors or in other potentially dirty environments. To avoid excessive damage and risk consequent loss of data, it is worth protecting the sheets by enclosing them within plastic sleeves, coating them in plastic laminate or waterproofing them with a suitable waterproofing or waxing agent. Alternatively, paper can be replaced altogether by another material such as acetate. As well as simple protection record forms will also require security. This means that they do not blow away, fall apart or become muddled with the first draught that they encounter.

The practical aim of efficient record-keeping is a simple one: it enables you, as an experimenter, to continually monitor the experiment and data collection at as high a level as possible. It enables you to keep a general overview of the running of the experiment without getting bogged down in continual back-checking, cross-referencing and paper shuffling. It really does make life a lot smoother.

Once back at your department the field data should be transferred to a master log. This log will contain the data from all observations made under all conditions and variables. This master log usually takes the form of a table. It may be a large or small, single or multi-paged. Here you will not only have all your data in one place but the data will be structured for ease of reference.

There are today a number of computer database packages available which are excellent for setting up a master log. By all means use these but always keep a separate hard copy print-out. Preferably keep two copies – one for use and one for security. This means, of course, that you do not keep both hard copies together in the same place! The reason for keeping a separate copy of your master log is both obvious and frequently overlooked. Suffice it to say that you would not be the first to have had data 'dumped' by a system, or to have had a data disc or two disappear. Having to re-load, re-check and correct 3000 data points from a master log (as was the case in one study when a disc went missing) is not good for one's morale, but it is not as soul destroying an activity as having to return to first principles, and flush the data out from the initial raw test sheets for want of a structured master log. Furthermore, you must give your storage space a little thought. The author once came across a researcher who kept his master log in the same filing cabinet drawer as his confidential waste paper. The inevitable happened! If using a computer disc to hold your data then ensure you make a back-up disc which is regularly updated. Storing results on a computer database does have the advantage that they can be more easily transferred across programs for statistical analysis without the trouble of keying in afresh all the data points.

How long after the experiment should these data be kept? That depends. Most students will throw their records away once their experimental write-up or report has been marked. More rigid experimentalists will say that experimental logs and data are *never* thrown away and certainly the experimental diaries of erstwhile scientists still make fascinating reading today. Others, the author has heard tell, store their data for between three and five years due primarily to the problems of storage and archiving. There have even been times when certain data items have had to be destroyed as soon as they were transcribed. For example, on one occasion, as part of a field experiment, it was necessary to collect the personal histories and various individual characteristics from a specialist group within the armed forces. The collection of this material was agreed to by the military but only on the condition that all the original forms and personal identifiers were shredded as soon as the raw data had been sanitized and transcribed, in purely numerical form to the master log. It is obvious that in such instances you must be very clear about what data are needed and you must ensure that these are obtained first time around as it will be impossible to return to the original point of collection. Such circumstances as these are rare but they do exist.

Finally, the case for systematic and structured records cannot be over-emphasized. Without clear records the student will have difficulty in analysing the data and writing up the experimental report. Without clear records it will be impossible to pursue related lines of research, which may arise in the future, without re-running the original trials. Inadequate collection and collation of data is a very common cause of delay in writing up dissertations and theses.

SAQ 16
What can you do to improve the efficiency of your data processing?

Summary of section 20

1 Good office organization is essential for successful data collection, logging, collation and analysis. Good organization:
   (a) reduces the workload on the experimenter;
   (b) reduces unnecessary administrative pressure on the subjects;
   (c) produces an efficient atmosphere in which to work.
2 Enforce a discipline and structure onto your data.
3 Capture experimental data as close to the source as possible and enter them into structured record forms.
4 Copy all data from the record forms to a master log. If using a computerized database then ensure you have a hard-copy print-out of all the raw data.
5 Data security. Keep a second copy of your data log in a separate secure place. If using a computer disc then ensure you have a back-up disc which is regularly updated.

21   *The Write Up*

A project or scientific experiment usually finishes with a *write up*. It may be a paper for submission to a scientific journal or a student project in whole or part submission for a degree or other qualification, or it might be an in-house document.

It is not the intention here to describe how psychology reports should be written and presented, that is left to other texts (see *Designing and Reporting Experiments*, by Peter Harris). Rather it is proposed to briefly address a few of the issues which frequently confront students when they come to start writing reports.

It is fair to say that report writing is seen as a chore. It is a burden which is to be put off for as long as possible. Sometimes it is left just that bit too long, resulting in the submission of reports which are obviously rushed and frequently shabby and this is usually accompanied by pleas for submission dates to be extended. Wanton procrastination means that completion of the report becomes urgent and this urgency comes to dominate other important activities, such as revision for examinations. A good experiment can suffer in a bad report. And there is no point in doing yourself a disservice.

Let us briefly consider some of the more common reasons why students delay in writing reports. In many instances the belief that writing experimental reports is drudgery has been instilled at school. The fun is in the laboratory, the report is an unfortunate appendage left for homework, much like a punishment. Also some students dislike or are even afraid of criticism and, as they expect their report to be criticized, will try to delay the event for as long as possible. This, of course, is a classic case of denial. The student starts believing that the deadline will never arrive. Other students seek a level of perfection in their work which they are frightened they will not attain. Consequently, they dare not make any start which might commit them to producing something less than perfect. This condition is also known to be a common problem underlying writer's block generally, and the reason why some artists will spend hours staring at a blank canvas. They are afraid of the personal commitment to which their first stroke binds them.

Another false belief, prevalent particularly amongst new students, is that to write a report one starts at the beginning and works systematically towards the end. This, as all experienced report writers know, is not the case at all. In fact, the two sections of a report which are most commonly written last are the *Abstract* and the *Introduction*. Reports and papers divide into natural sections, and these sections can be tackled independently as and when appropriate. For instance, you should write up a description of the *Method* and *Results* sections first while you remember the details, adding the more theoretical *Introduction* and *Discussion* later to ensure that they lead on from your results.

Another common failing when producing a report is to underestimate the amount of time required to prepare diagrams, tables, appendices, front and end matter such as title pages, contents lists, foreword and so on. Many writers think of a report as solely the body of the text while the additions are mere niceties which can be sprinkled in at the last moment. In reality, a good 30% of report writing time can be spent on these additions.

There is also the fallacy, again rather prevalent among students, that reports are written. Of course they are not. Reports are always *re*-written. The first time pen is applied to paper is to produce a draft. The report itself comes later after various amounts of chopping, stuffing and cobbling have taken place. The re-writing may require more than one draft to be produced before all that is needed is a final tightening up of the nuts and bolts of the report.

The student who has prepared an experimental plan, drawn up a functional specification, has kept a project diary and has the data and results safely logged, should have little trouble in producing a report. Most of the work will already have been done. All that remains is to distil the information into the appropriate format and style for a specific audience. To be truthful though, a certain amount of effort will always be demanded of the writer. It helps if you accept that the job has to be done anyway, tackle it head on, and have the first draft written up as early as possible. Remember to build up your reserve time.

It is important to include the time needed for writing your report into the experimental plan. Assess how much time you will need to write the report then multiply that figure by three (to produce the *document*), next insert that figure into your plan and you will see how little time you really have to run your project!

To put some actual figures on report writing the Science and Engineering Research Council arrived at the following times to completion of a PhD thesis which is admittedly a three or four year project, rather than the six-month project more commonly found in undergraduate courses, but the lesson is the same (Christopherson *et al.*, 1983):

Introduction	3 weeks
Method and results	6 weeks
Discussion, tables, figures references, etc.	6 weeks
Typing	2 weeks
Consultation with supervisor	1 week
Revision of draft	2 weeks
Final typing, art work, figures, proof reading, etc.	3 weeks
Binding	1 week

Total   24 weeks

You will notice that these figures do not include time for analysis, background reading or work other than producing the report.

For many people today, writing is an operational requirement and those, like students, who need to write would find it useful to train themselves to be able to do three things: firstly, they should be able to write *when* they want. It is no use waiting for inspiration. It never comes when it is needed. Secondly, they should train themselves to write for long periods at a stretch. Short bursts of frantic activity are of no use to anyone. Rather the writer should be able to provide a sustained and relaxed output. Thirdly, it is worth the effort in training to develop the ability to write anywhere at all – on trains, in canteens, at airports, in cars, in a ditch if necessary. So much of our lives drift away in such places (well, perhaps not in ditches for most people) that trying to salvage something constructive from them can be a real asset. Naturally, the writing produced under such conditions is not expected to be of final manuscript quality. Even rough notes will suffice – providing that you simply write. One note of encouragement: report writing does become easier with practice – but there again the reports do seem to grow longer as well!

Effective report writing is a crucial skill for the applied experimental psychologist. Unlike most of their laboratory-based colleagues, applied scientists have to communicate their results routinely to people with no scientific, and especially no psychological, training. When writing technical documents it helps to bear constantly in mind that few people in this world actually like having to read reports. *No-one* likes having to read reports twice.

Summary of section 21

1 All experiments and projects finish with a written report. This enables your findings to be passed into the public domain.
2 There are various reasons for students failing to submit an adequate report on time, among the most common of which are:
   (a) A view that a report is merely an addendum, or afterthought, to the study and consequently of little significance.
   (b) A belief at the beginning of the study that the deadline for submitting a report is too far away to bother about planning. This is denial compounded by an inability to estimate time.
   (c) A fear of criticism.
   (d) A striving after unrealistic perfection and anxiety about being committed to something less than perfect.
   (e) A belief that one must write a report by starting at the beginning and working through to the end. In practice the report should be broken down into naturally manageable chunks and each treated independently.
   (f) A gross underestimation of the time required to write a report. Time to produce diagrams, tables, references, appendices, etc. is frequently underestimated.
   (g) The closely-held belief that reports are actually written, when in truth they are always re-written.
3 Prepare an experimental plan, draw up a functional specification and keep a project diary and the report is already 80% written.
4 Applied experimental psychologists (and others whose lives will involve much report writing) would do well to train themselves to be able to:
   (a) write when they want to;
   (b) write for long periods at a stretch;
   (c) write anywhere at all.
5 Effective report writing is a fundamental skill for the applied psychologist because of the need to communicate routinely with non-psychologists. No-one likes having to read reports twice.

22 Decommissioning the Experiment

Once the experiment has been carried out, the data analysed, and the report handed in, most students are then content to call it a day. With field work however, there are always a few outstanding items which need to be cleared up and, as any craftsman will tell you, a job is never finished until all rubbish has been cleared away and all tools cleaned and stowed. The problem of clearing away an experiment should always be addressed with the larger postgraduate projects but the principle remains the same at all levels. In effect you have to deliberately *decommission* your project. This may sound rather grandiose but it simply means tying up all the loose ends in a methodical manner. The following are the most important factors which need to be considered.

22.1 Data security

Ensure that all your data are stored somewhere secure and that all the variables and numbers can be referenced easily at a later date. That is, do not mark your variables 'X', 'Y' or 'Z' but give them names which are meaningful. You will soon forget what 'X', 'Y' or 'Z' stood for. If your data are written on more than one sheet of paper then it is essential to ensure that the data are easy to cross-reference between the pages. The data log should have enough inherent information to stand alone without the need to refer to other documents to understand it. You will be surprised at how frequently in the future that you will want to check back to some data from an old experiment.

22.2 Acknowledgements

You must write to your host organization and subjects and thank them for their support and participation. This is frequently overlooked and it does the reputation of the applied experimentalist no good at all. You will normally have liaised with one key person within the host organization, so send this individual a complementary copy of your paper or report after your letter of thanks. It is not usually necessary to write to each subject who took part in your study individually, but they do appreciate being remembered. A letter on headed paper, for the organization's noticeboard and/or an inclusion in the company newsletter is always welcome. Along with a copy of the report itself you should always send a separate summary which is written in language for the layman. You must remember that your final report is a technical document written for an audience invariably different from that of your host organization. A summary of your findings on no more than one page is often appreciated. Keep it simple but do not insult their intelligence.

You might also return to the host organization either to give a presentation of your study or to discuss your findings. The host organization has, after all, committed its resources to your experiment, and it is only natural that they would be interested in your findings. It is also natural, by the very nature of your study, that your findings may be of direct relevance to the functioning of the organization itself. Try to clear this obligation out of the way as soon as possible. The longer you leave it the more difficult it becomes to fulfil. The best approach is to consider this task as an experimental debriefing session and build it into your plan. By doing that you have acknowledged the task as a natural part of your study.

22.3   Matériel

Equipment should be returned to the various quarters whence it came. Work methodically through the checklists and make up any deficiencies in material which have occurred. You are then ready to start intact and afresh on the next project.

Finally, *kill* your project. Some students find that a few strands of their study will continue to drag on for far too long. These strands suck an unnecessary amount of energy and resources from other projects including other entirely new experiments. You should work out the steps needed to run down the project after submission of the report, and set a deadline by which time they are to be completed. Once the decommissioning is achieved then acknowledge that the study is dead, let it go, and move on to fresher pastures.

Summary of section 22

1 A study is not finished when the final report is written but when all tools, materials and duties have been cleared away.
2 In the larger research studies the decommissioning of a project is a major undertaking which needs to be planned for and should be approached methodically.
3 Three important factors to be considered when running down a project are:
   (a) *Data security*. Store all data securely and ensure that they can be easily understood at a later date.

(b) *Acknowledgements*. Do thank your hosts, subjects and anyone else who had an input into your project.

(c) *Matériel*. All equipment should be repaired (if necessary), re-supplied and returned to its rightful place.

4 Finally, *kill* your project. You must let it go.

Part 5
Lessons from Field Research

Practice is the best of all instructors.

Publilius

Experience is a dear teacher, but fools will learn at no other.
Poor Richard's Almanac

Introduction

Any experimental study conducted within an external organization or setting will present the experimenter with certain issues which, although peripheral to the study, are important and need to be addressed. Four of the more common factors include firstly, the often subtle effects the experimenter may have on his or her subjects, effects which can bias the experimental results. Secondly, ethical implications, often important, have a sharper relief in field research. Thirdly, organizational politics pervades any group and the experimenter is bound to meet it at some point. Any experimenter will need to work hard to avoid becoming enmeshed in its web. Finally, how will you be perceived by the very people you want to use as subjects?

These four factors are considered in more detail below. They are deliberately grouped into a separate section for ease of reference by the reader and in keeping with the aim of using this book as a *field manual* rather than the more straightforward textbook.

23   The Hawthorne Effect

In 1927 Professor Elton Mayo at Harvard University began an essentially simple field experiment which was conducted on site at the Hawthorne works of the Western Electric Company. The experiment was concerned with the effect of different levels of illumination on performance at three different tasks: inspecting small engineering parts, winding electrical coils and assembling electrical relays. This experiment had far-reaching consequences.

The experimental design was straightforward enough: the experimental groups worked under four different levels of illumination while the control groups continued to work, as usual, under the already existing factory lights. The results showed that task performance in the experimental groups improved with increased illumination. This may not come as too much of a surprise. The intriguing point, however, was that the performance of the *control* groups also improved significantly.

Here was a problem. After all, the whole *raison d'être* of a control group is that it does not behave like an experimental group. That is to say, it does not unless the hypothesis is flawed.

113

The experimenters then set up a second study in which the experimental design was more refined. This time there was only one experimental and one control group. The subjects in each group were matched for job experience and average rate of production. This also meant, of course, that there were equal numbers of subjects in each group. The experimental group worked under three different light intensities, while the control group worked under constant illumination. The groups were physically separated, each one working in a different building. Once again the results showed that the performance of both the experimental and control groups improved significantly, and that they did so to an almost identical degree.

So it was back to the drawing board. More refinements were made to the third experiment: this time only artificial light was used, while daylight was excluded altogether for both groups. The control group worked under a constant intensity of 10 foot-candles (107.6 lux), while the experimental group worked under an initial intensity of 10 foot-candles, which was decreased over successive periods by 1 foot-candle (10.76 lux) intervals until the intensity reached 3 foot-candles (32.28 lux). Despite this fall off in illumination to a level of discomfort, the experimental group *still* maintained its original level of efficiency.

By now things were beginning to become a little extreme. The fourth experiment involved two women who volunteered to undergo trials in a light-controlled room in which the light intensity was decreased to the level of ordinary moonlight! At this level the subjects were able to maintain production. They also told the experimenters that they had no eye strain and even felt less fatigued than when working under brighter lights. They preferred the dimmer lights.

In the fifth experiment, the light intensity was increased steadily every day. The women reported that they liked the brighter lights. There was no difference in the level of performance.

At this stage many experimentalists would have thrown in the towel. It is to the credit of both the experimenters and the Western Electric Company, that they, after a radical re-think of what they were investigating, continued their studies. These Hawthorne studies were to take 12 years to complete and involve a total of five distinct projects.

It is not possible to consider the rest of these studies in further detail here. There are some good detailed summary accounts of the research in print, which the prospective field experimenter is recommended to read. They should be read for the insight they give into running applied psychology experiments and the description of various types of problems which still arise in field studies today. Read them as one would read any other classic, for a classic of practical experimentation they undoubtedly are. The main point which is highlighted by the Hawthorne studies is that, in certain circumstances, the experimenters may themselves become an extraneous variable in the experiment. In other words, the performance of people in their natural settings may be altered by the mere fact that someone is paying attention to them and that their work then takes on a greater degree of importance. Motivational factors can easily arise in the field experiment and these will need to be identified and controlled. The Hawthorne studies also indicate that there are limits to the 'subject-in-isolation' approach to experimentation – an approach which is pursued in many laboratories today. They also indicate that the life of an applied experimental psychologist can be a tough one!

Although the Hawthorne studies still have relevance for us today they are not without criticism. They are not perfect and some aspects show a certain naïvety which is quite alien in contemporary research, for example, the differences between two sets of results could be because one group was composed solely of men and the other of women.

Nonetheless, part of the inherent beauty of the Hawthorne research is that the experimenters were brave enough to confront their rather frustrating data head on, and pursued their results, irrespective of where they led, in an undirected search after the confounding variables.

Summary of section 23

1 A field experiment often involves the researcher paying special attention to his or her subjects. The findings of the Hawthorne studies and more recent social psychological research has shown that this attention can itself significantly bias the results of the experiment.
2 The social implications of the Hawthorne studies throw into question the principle of treating each subject as though he or she existed in total isolation. That, in practice, a subject will respond to friends, colleagues, bosses and the experimenter in varying and subtle ways.

24   Ethical Factors in Behavioural Research

All behavioural research carries ethical implications and field research seems to carry rather more of a day-to-day nature than laboratory-based studies. This is more a consequence of the diversity of the people and the environments within which the studies are conducted, rather than for any other reason.

The question of ethics in experimentation is one which tends to befuddle psychology students at some stage or other in their course of study. Often these questions are unnecessary and much time can be lost in a fruitless witch-hunt for non-existent problems. Much of this difficulty lies in attempting to consider ethics purely in the abstract. This should be left to philosophers. Ethics is a very practical subject, and once a practical approach is adopted much of the confusion disappears.

Most ethical 'problems' are essentially simple to resolve but they need to be resolved early. Providing the physical and psychological well-being of your subject is put above all else, followed closely by the integrity of your discipline and yourself, few things will cause real conflict. Nonetheless, there are a few issues which arise quite commonly in behavioural research and which the student will encounter quite early in his or her career. These are now considered in more detail below.

24.1   Deception

The question of deception in behavioural research is one which is raised frequently. Deception is but one form of clandestine activity, others include eavesdropping, the deliberate manipulation of people and probing into an individual's personal affairs and backgrounds. Some will argue that the use of such methods and the concomitant invasion of personal privacy is ethically untenable. Others (for example Brandt, 1972) would argue that clandestine techniques are not only right and proper but indeed are essential for furthering behavioural research in natural settings.

In reality the need to use deception arises very rarely and then it is found predominantly among the social psychology studies. In applied behavioural research, you will find that far from needing to deceive your subjects you will often be able to tell them precisely what you and your experiment are about without compromising your study in any way.

Do bear in mind that practices such as deception can backfire with painful consequences for both the subject and the experimenter. It is the subject who always suffers most. People do not like being deceived and they most certainly do not like discovering that they have been deceived. Among other things it destroys their self-respect and their sense of personal dignity. The subject realizes that for a while he or she has personally lost control of the situation. They feel betrayed and betrayal hurts.

As a rule of thumb, if planning to deceive your subjects, ask yourself whether you are performing an experiment or a conjuring trick.

24.2   *Fear*

Stress, fear and anxiety are sometimes induced in subjects as an independent variable. The three common sources of stress are *physical, physiological* and *psychological*.

24.2.1   *Physical stress*
Physical stress commonly arises from environmental conditions such as extremes of heat, cold, pressure and so on.

24.2.2   *Physiological stress*
Physiological stress can be induced by, for example, extremes of fatigue, exhaustion, as well as pharmacological agents, food and drink deprivation, etc.

24.2.3   *Psychological stress*
Psychological stress arises when the subject is, or genuinely believes himself to be, in a threatening situation.

In certain circumstances, inculcating stress, fear or anxiety is perfectly legitimate. For example, researchers have investigated the psychological and physiological correlates of stress and anxiety during free-fall parachuting, racing driving, military operations, deep sea diving, post-coronary care, phobic conditions and many others. A high level of fear or stress in subjects is unacceptable when it is no more than a by-product of the experiment. To many subjects even entering a psychological laboratory can produce anxiety.

Before leaving fear it is important to realize that, as well as the three sources of fear mentioned above (physical, physiological and psychological) there exists a very powerful and often overlooked fourth source. This is the fear which is brought about by the violation of a person's ideas and beliefs. Such violations can arise when undertaking research into areas which society considers taboo such as certain types and extremes of sensual behaviour and even death. In its day the Masters and Johnson (1966) survey into the everyday sexual mores of Americans caused an outcry because it penetrated what was then a taboo area and threatened the beliefs people held about their own society's behaviour. Taboos are flexible and today such a survey would be considered quite tame.

24.3   *Informed consent*

In an ideal world your subjects would understand what your study was about and on this understanding would readily consent to take part. In practice this level of informed consent is rarely possible. There are two difficulties with truly informed consent – *bias* and *naïvety*:

24.3.1   Bias
There are occasions when fully describing your experiment to your subjects can lead to a biased sample. Obviously, should your sample become biased then the ability to generalize from the sample to the overall population becomes, at least to an extent, compromised.

24.3.2   Naïvety
In most applied experiments in behavioural research your subject sample will be drawn from people inhabiting the real world. It is a characteristic of these people that they are, on the whole, scientifically naïve. It is, therefore, simply not possible to obtain *fully* informed consent from a scientifically, and especially psychologically, naïve audience. You will find that you can explain the workings of your experiment up to a point but beyond that point your subjects must put their trust in you.

24.4   Trust

It is fair to say that the lay public do not really understand either the workings of science or scientists themselves. Fortunately, although the public do not understand scientists they do trust them, or at least are prepared to give them the benefit of the doubt. Ethically nothing must be done in the name of research which would compromise this trust. There is a difficulty here in that behavioural research can be prone to being misconstrued and the very nature of its psychological intervention and enquiry means that the trust rendered by the public is a fragile one. The consequences of breaching this trust is a severe curtailment on the freedom to pursue research.

24.5   Corruption

Ethically the scientist is obliged to eschew and prevent corruption. There exist two main categories of corruption which need to be guarded against – *experimenter bias* and *misrepresentation*.

24.5.1   Experimenter bias
Researchers go to much trouble to develop an hypothesis and it soon becomes adopted as one of the family with the consequence that they are reluctant to see it come to any harm. People are naturally loathe to murder

their own babies. They will order events to help them. Major scientific fraud is, fortunately, rare but one must be on the guard against experimental weaknesses which can bias a result in one direction or another. A researcher, for example, may settle for an experimental design which is not as rigorous as it could be; a statistical analysis is employed which may not be quite the most appropriate test or measurements may be recorded to a false level of accuracy and then arbitrarily rounded up or down. The experimenter has a feeling for which way the data *ought* to go and this feeling can pervade subtly and insidiously the manner in which the study is conducted. It must be emphasized that such bias usually creeps in unwittingly and the innocent researcher, once aware of the situation, would be the first to prohibit such influence.

Many students become ensnared in the power of their pet hypothesis and are reluctant to let it go completely despite the evidence. This bias is seen regularly in laboratory reports where the student will imply that if the result is non-significant then there has to be something wrong with the experimental design, the procedure, the sample population or indeed anything except that their carefully nurtured hypothesis should prove false. If there are so many genuine criticisms of an experiment then why carry it out in the first place?

Use the strongest experimental design possible and the most appropriate analysis and all major experimenter bias will be eliminated.

24.5.2   Misrepresentation

It is a sad fact of our times that misrepresentation of scientific information is a constant threat. The biggest threat comes not from scientists themselves but from the worlds of journalism, advertising and politics. It is true that there are people in these professions who genuinely wish to inform the public on matters of science and science policy. It is also true that there exist those whose aim is not to inform but to persuade and scientific information can be twisted to support their arguments.

It must also be said that there are journalists and reporters who again seek not to inform but to sensationalize. They need a story to sell and it is the sensational stories which sell copy. It does happen that scientific accounts are published which have had certain features exaggerated and others left out. The story published may not be the story presented. It also happens that the journalist's interpretation of the facts may not be quite accurate.

Misrepresentation may occur quite innocently. A journalist attempting to communicate matters of science to an audience which is on the whole poorly educated scientifically has a major task ahead. There is a need to reduce quite complex scientific issues to simple elements the essence of which can be readily grasped by the layman. These issues present themselves in many colours, hues, tones and shades but to be understood by the non-expert they need to be presented in black and white. In so doing one carries the risk of producing major distortion. Science is a discipline which does not allow for premature understanding.

It is incumbent upon the scientific world to aid the genuine journalists and reporters in their efforts to communicate scientific issues fairly to the lay public. Both groups are responsible for preventing the abuse of science by hacks. Psychology and medicine, because they touch the everyday lives of people, are particularly prone to journalistic use and abuse. A little misrepresentation can destroy a great deal of trust. You must be on your guard to prevent any such misrepresentation of your research. This *is* an ethical issue.

24.6   Confidentiality

All data and personal information are confidential. You guard these with the seal of the confessional. The confidentiality of personal data and the maintenance of subject anonymity are the overriding principles of subject welfare. Confidentiality is discussed further in section 18.3 on real subjects. Along with confidentiality comes *anonymity*. You must maintain anonymity of your subjects at all times.

24.7   Risk

Certain areas of research involve an element of risk to the subject, for example hazardous activities and professions such as diving, flying, soldiering as well as drug taking and so on. When designing an experiment which possesses a degree of personal risk for your subject ask yourself the following questions:

- Will your experiment harm the subject? Remember that harm can arise from physical, physiological or psychological causes.
- How essential is your study? Asking your subjects to shoulder some personal risk for an experiment which is essentially trivial is unacceptable.
- Can your experiment be achieved by any other means? If not, is it still ethically acceptable? It may be that the problem you are attempting to solve by experiment is scientifically ahead of its time.

There are instances when risk is acceptable to your subject, but it must not be undue risk.

For the applied experimental psychologist ethics is not a metaphysical discourse. It is a very practical issue. This is not to dismiss ethics; on the contrary, ethics in research is a subject of fundamental importance. It is not, however, one which is peculiar to research psychologists. Doctors, nurses, police officers, social workers, priests, lawyers and even accountants frequently face problems of an ethical nature. The very substance of behavioural research, however, can pose distinct problems for the experimenter and the reader is referred to the relevant ethical guidelines which have been drawn up by various bodies and particularly the revised code of Ethical Principles for Conducting Research with Human Participants produced by the British Psychological Society and which is here reprinted with permission in Appendix 1.

Finally, any persistent or recurring ethical problems should be discussed in the first instance with your supervisor. If you find that after these discussions there still remains an unresolved issue in your study then refer the matter to an Ethics Committee for official review. Most universities and polytechnics will have such a committee, or at least will have access to one through perhaps the local general hospital. If submitting an experiment to an Ethics Committee it is worth bearing in mind three points:

- Firstly, ensure that there is someone on the committee who is familiar at least with your discipline. If you are proposing to use a specific experimental technique in your research there should be someone on the board who knows precisely what is involved in that technique and its implications. You have the right to insist upon such representation.
- Secondly, remember that an Ethics Committee is still at heart a committee, so do not expect an early response. This will have implications for your project plans.
- Thirdly, remember that Ethics Committees are there to help you conduct your research, not to hinder you. Do not be afraid to seek their advice.

Summary of section 24

1 Ethics in research is a fundamental issue. All behavioural research carries ethical implications and field research carries more than most.
2 Fortunately, in practice major ethical concerns are few and often simple to resolve.
3 Few difficulties will be encountered providing you:
  (a) put the physical and psychological well-being of your subjects above all else;
  (b) maintain the integrity of your discipline;
  (c) maintain the scientific and personal integrity of yourself;
  (d) eschew deception wherever possible;
  (e) always maintain confidentiality of data and personal information;

(f) always maintain the anonymity of your subjects.

4 If in doubt refer the matter to an appropriate Ethics Committee for review and advice.

25   *Politics*

Organizational or company politics are a bane from which most people try to escape. Sometimes, even with the best will in the world, it cannot be done. Politics are everywhere and the field experimenter should keep a wary eye open to avoid being sucked into the maelstrom. This is not always easy and one can be caught out quite innocently. A common trap, for example, is that of being used by one faction to wage war on another. For instance, in one company, whose share price had dropped to its lowest level for many years and was subsequently in some difficulty, a research psychologist found himself being used as a sounding board by each of the company's departments to berate the other departments. This may not seem too onerous at first glance but consider how you should respond; do you agree with any person's views or disagree with them or perhaps you signify 'no comment', but how will that be interpreted? In another experiment and in a different company, a psychologist accidentally uncovered an underlying group tension which had been simmering for some time, and which now erupted into friction between his control and experimental groups. He eventually had to abort his experiment because the morale of the whole workforce was suffering.

The applied psychologist may also find that some subjects will unload onto them personal grievances about their management, workforce, supervisors, and/or colleagues. As an applied psychologist you must be very careful how you respond to such revelations. It is all too easy to say something which you may consider to be simply neutral and friendly, but which is taken by the other party as acquiescence and even support for their 'cause'. Any views which you express will certainly be used to bolster individual factions. It can help to say simply that you are unable to comment upon such matters.

For the most part you will be welcomed by the people in the host organization because you have some novelty and can provide a break in their routine. At other times you may be received with mistrust and perhaps even open hostility. If you do find such resistance it is often because you are being seen as a management 'tool'. Do not be too concerned about such hostility; the most common explanation for it is that your subjects distrust their own management. Perhaps in any one instance they are right to do so, perhaps not. The point is that such reactions are unlikely to help you in your study. Incidentally, wherever there is distrust of management it is well to check how effective is their control and communication, especially the latter (see section 4.5).

It does not matter who your subjects are, you will want them on your side. It helps therefore if you are not only independent and impartial, but are seen to be so. Ensure you hold no partiality to any one department or group. Coming into an organization under a university, polytechnic or college banner certainly helps by implying a degree of independence and impartiality. Explaining to the people in the organization in simple and clear terms precisely what you are doing and why is a tremendous asset in smoothing your path.

There are other reasons for encountering possible mistrust. You must appreciate that you are unlikely to be the only 'outsider' to have been presented to your subjects. Business analysts, auditors, management consultants, computer systems analysts, accountants, factory inspectors, health officers can all appear briefly on the scene and all will invariably pose a threat to the routine of your subjects by leaving a blaze of change in their wake. Occupational psychologists and the new breed of 'business psychologists' are also included amongst these peripatetic functionaries.

There may of course be genuine reasons for any feelings of mistrust which you might encounter. The author has it on good authority that one experimenter was welcomed onto a work site by the management because they had suspected for some time that one particular group of employees was regularly cheating the organization and it was hoped that the experimenter would be able to shed some light on this practice. The experimenter, of course, was not told of these machinations. The author has also been informed that one company paid for a team of computer experts ostensibly to carry out a systems analysis of the company's functions, but in reality to try to expose an area of suspected fraud. Again the analysts were not told of the real intentions of the company and these were only discovered later on by accident. One of the analysts remarked, perhaps understandably, that this particular incident had left a bad taste in his mouth.

Finally, do not pay heed to the frequent moans and complaints about whichever organization you are working in, be it business, industry, the services and so on. It is the common lot of people to grumble: it is when the grumbling stops that the organization needs to worry.

The existence of organizational politics cannot be denied. For the most part they will present no problem at all to the experimenter but there are times when you may accidentally expose a raw nerve. If you keep on the quiet *qui vive* for political undertones and determine to keep out of them at all costs there should be little problem in carrying out your experiment. Above all, do not let yourself be used by one faction to score points against another, and never allow yourself to be sent in on the sly to sort out a company's own problems. It is a sad reflection that, although rare, these things do happen.

Summary of section 25

1 'Company politics' are inherent in any organization. For the most part you will avoid them easily enough.
2 Be alert for group friction which may exist between different departments or sections, or between management and staff.
3 Do not allow yourself or your project to be used by one faction against another.
4 Common sense and a sinew of humour will see you through comfortably.

26   A Subject's Eye View of the Psychologist

A few words about the subject's eye view of the experimenter would not come amiss. It is fair to say that most people you will encounter have not knowingly come across a psychologist before and consequently you will have some novelty value. Many of those that you meet will think of a psychologist as being a psychiatrist and hence a medically qualified doctor or even a psychoanalyst. This perception can be compounded if you happen to possess an academic doctorate (a PhD). If you are not careful you can leave yourself wide open to being misused. Either, one of your subjects will want to unload their back problem onto you (or worse their domestic problems) or someone will grab you by the arm and insist that you look at poor Joe who is sitting on the floor looking very dazed and holding a broken arm. Just as an aside, the most frequent incidents that the author has been called on to look at have been eye injuries: infections, chemical burns, arch eye, etc. Surprisingly, many people who should know better will also tend to think of you as a man or woman of medicine, e.g. graduates and postgraduates from other disciplines such as engineering. One cannot help feeling that a study into the public's perception of psychologists is long overdue.

As far as the people you are dealing with are concerned (that is, your subjects and others in the host organization) you are of a professional standing and will be expected to conduct yourself as a member of the professional classes – by both the workforce and the management of your host organization. This is not a straitjacket; you should still possess your individual freedom and character. It is not unknown for some students, male and female, to try to act as 'one of the boys' with their subjects when clearly not so. This approach often backfires. Your subjects will see through your act very quickly and they will alienate you. Fortunately, psychology does tend to be a subject to which people are drawn after having worked in other occupations or professions, e.g. armed forces, civil engineering, the legal profession, train driving, etc. There is no doubt that such a background can be a tremendous asset.

Summary of section 26

1 Be prepared to be misperceived. As an experimental psychologist you can still find yourself being mistaken for a psychiatrist or even a psychoanalyst in the mind of the general public.
2 You will be seen as a member of the professional classes and will be expected to conduct yourself as such.
3 Do not try to muck in with your subjects by attempting to act as 'one of the boys'. It will backfire.

Part 6
Project Management Techniques for Field Research

For Art and Science cannot exist but in minutely organised Particulars.
WILLIAM BLAKE (1757–1827)

27   *Managing the Experiment*

Every experiment, every research project is unique. What they have in common is that each experiment and project involves change. Project management tools exist to manage, monitor and control this change. Whether a project comprises one experiment or many the necessary controls must be applied to ensure a successful outcome. A successful outcome does not mean that a statistically significant result is obtained, but that the experimental programme runs to plan and within the time and budgetary constraints laid down. It is not enough just to plan an experiment, that plan must also be controlled. This section deals with the preliminary concepts of project control, management and scheduling. This it does at a necessarily basic level.

Formal techniques for monitoring and controlling projects sprang into their own in the 1950s with a method known as *Critical path scheduling* which was developed independently by the Central Electricity Generating Board (England) and the United States Navy. Shortly afterwards a related method known as *Project evaluation and review technique* (PERT) generated much interest when its application to the Polaris missile project resulted in the programme being completed two years ahead of schedule and within budget. Today project management techniques have become very sophisticated and many require a substantial training period before they can be utilized effectively. In this text the emphasis will be confined to the simple but effective technique known as the *Gantt* or *bar chart*. Gantt charts can be used very quickly and are easy to grasp and build. The more advanced techniques, such as network scheduling, will not be covered although the interested reader is referred to the many good introductory texts on the subject which exist today. Before tackling the building blocks of the Gantt chart it is worth pausing to consider briefly the actual purpose behind formal project management and how such techniques can help the researcher to achieve his or her aim.

It is important at the outset to emphasize that project management techniques and schedules do not exist to rigidly 'fix' plans. They are not straitjackets on the programme, nor do they hamper scientific creativity. If used correctly, scheduling tools will actually release the researcher for more creative work.

In practice few projects can be expected to follow precisely the plan drawn up at the beginning of the study. In research this risk is increased manifold as witnessed by the number of PhD submissions whose content is substantially different from the original concepts and plans enthusiastically drawn up by the new postgraduate in those first heady few weeks of study. Deviations from the plan are to be expected. These deviations will arise through unforeseen events which, by definition, cannot be predicted. Consequently, any schedule must in reality always be a *draft*. It can never be anything more than a rough cast. Remembering this will prevent you from becoming frozen by the fear of being locked into a preset course which may take you down a wrong route with no possibility of correction. Although most deviations cannot be predicted, a schedule will enable them to be contained and controlled. The researcher can then quickly see where replanning is required. In order to ensure fast intervention and to facilitate rapid re-planning, it is necessary to have project information collection and reference methods which are both quick and simple. Some of the more relevant advantages of project management and scheduling techniques to the researcher are given below.

Evaluating. Scheduling techniques are useful in that they enable the researcher to evaluate an initial plan before committing himself to it. Furthermore, with a substantial research project, such as a two to four year Master or Doctor of Philosophy (MPhil or PhD), a selection of different plans would normally be drawn up and evaluated. Project management techniques enable the researcher to try out different ways of running the same project and to compare these easily, until the most effective approach is found.

Committing. Project management and scheduling techniques also function at a more human level. They are powerful persuaders in engendering a commitment to the experiment amongst those who are to be involved by demonstrating visually that the plan has been well thought out. They show that it is achievable.

Computing. Project management tools are ideally suited to computer analysis and many such project planners are currently available on the market.

Starting. A practical *start* date to a project can be aimed for with realistic confidence. Also, once a future start date has been established, it is much easier to schedule non-project activities, thus preventing clashes of interest once the study is under way.

Analysing. Formal schedules help to identify these critical factors in the project which will need a concentration of commitment and effort. The construction of a formal plan using standardized techniques forces the planner to carry out an analysis of the project in greater content and depth than would otherwise have been done.

Before continuing with a description of the Gantt chart it is important to be aware of the following dangers.

Firstly, do not fall into the trap of thinking that by merely using these techniques, all will go well with your project. Do not be seduced into believing that the application of sophisticated analysis will repair the fundamental flaws in your thinking. It will not. If the plan itself has been wrongly conceived or poorly thought through then all else is wasted effort.

SAQ 17
How can you help to eliminate flaws in your thinking at an early stage of planning?

Secondly, do not make any plan over-complicated. It is easy to do this simply because the means of complexity are available. All plans must be simple to comprehend and easy to respond to. This applies not only to the author of the plan but also to all those who will be participating in the project.

Thirdly, a plan constructed with project management tools is essential for the smooth running of any significant project. At some stage however, this plan must fuse with the real world. When it does, the discovery is readily made that a project, any project, cannot be run by mathematics alone. In applied psychological research especially, it will fall to the researcher to act as the coupling between the real world and the plan. There is no escaping this duty.

A schedule, in essence, provides a top-level description of the research project. One of the more common techniques for scheduling projects is described below.

Summary of section 27

1 Every research project is unique. They all involve change. Project management tools exist to monitor and control this change.
2 Project management techniques are not a straitjacket on a research programme. If properly applied they will actually allow the experimenter more freedom than he would otherwise have.
3 Deviations from a plan are to be expected; therefore, any schedule is always a draft.
4 Advantages of project management techniques to the researcher include:
   (a) a means for trying out on paper different ways of running the same project before selecting the most appropriate method;
   (b) engendering commitment in others by showing that a plan is achievable;
   (c) they are readily amenable to computer analysis;
   (d) a practical *start* date can be aimed for with a realistic confidence;
   (e) the researcher is forced to analyse his or her project to a greater level of detail than would otherwise have been the case.
5 Points to beware of:
   (a) no amount of project management will repair flawed thinking. If the plan itself has been wrongly conceived then all else is wasted;
   (b) do not be lured into making your plan over-complicated merely because you now have the means to do so;
   (c) at some stage you must couple your plan to the real world. You will now find that a plan cannot be run by mathematics alone.

28   *The Gantt Chart*

The Gantt chart (named after its inventor Henry Gantt) or bar chart as it is also known, is one of the simplest and most widely used methods of scheduling. A Gantt chart identifies all the main activities in a project, schedules them appropriately, shows their duration and gives the timing of each activity with respect to the others.

The primary function of the Gantt chart is to schedule activities against time. It is not generally used to schedule resources. Furthermore, the full interdependence of activities is not shown. Consequently, in a large project when unforeseen events strike, and the plan is forced to deviate, it may be difficult to determine its follow-on effects on other activities. Despite these criticisms, however, the Gantt chart is an extremely useful scheduling tool, applicable to many student research programmes, and whose use will repay the researcher manifold.

An example of a Gantt chart designed for a student field project is shown in Figure 6.1. It will be seen that all the key activities have been identified and listed in order of dependence, that is, those activities which must be completed before another activity can commence are listed first, see Table 6.1. These activities are then translated into a Gantt chart with the bars drawn against duration of activity. Some activities will be able to begin before another activity is finished, for example, in Figure 6.1 it is possible to begin activity: *construct experimental equipment* before identifying which organization will provide your subjects. It is unlikely to be possible, however, to commence experimental trials until all the equipment has been collected.

28.1   *Critical path*

Some activities may be carried out in parallel, some may not. Running through the plan will be a series of activities, any variation in which (e.g. a delay to their starting) will affect the whole project. Such activities are therefore, critical to the effectiveness and successful implementation of the whole plan. These critical activities should be identified and linked together into an activity chain. This chain is known as the critical path. Once the critical path has been established it is easy to see just how much time will be needed for your project. You will not be able to complete the project in less time than that shown by the critical path. Once this path has been identified then resources and resource allocations can be reappraised.

Identifying a critical path is not as difficult as it may at first appear. For

Table 6.1   List of key activities and durations

Serial	Activity	Duration
1	Background research	9 weeks
2	Initial experimental design	1 week
3	Identify resources	1 week
4	Contact host organization	4 weeks
5	Order proprietary equipment	5 weeks
6	Construct experimental equipment	5 weeks
7	Confirm pilot subject pool	4 weeks
8	Confirm subject pool	4 weeks
9	Run pilot study	1 week
10	Final experimental design	1 week
11	Move kit to site 1	2 days
12	Experimental trial 1	2 days
13	Log data	2 weeks
14	Move kit to site 2	2 days
15	Experimental trial 2	2 days
16	Decommission experiment	4 weeks
17	Analyse data	2 weeks
18	Prepare draft report	4 weeks
19	Prepare final report	4 weeks
20	Submit report and presentation	1 week

example, consider that your project has the following five activities, A, B, C, D, E, which are represented in Gantt chart form in Figure 6.2. From your activity table you know the following information:

Durations
   A 3 weeks
   B 8 weeks
   C 3 weeks
   D 3 weeks
   E 2 weeks
Activity A must be started first.
Activities B, C, D and E must therefore, follow A.
Activities A, B, C and D must be completed before E.
Activity C must be completed before D.

From the above and Figure 6.2 it can be seen that to complete the project in 13 weeks the start and finish dates for activities A, B, and E are fixed. The start and finish dates for activities C and D, on the other hand, can vary by two weeks *without affecting the completion time of the project*. This two weeks flexibility is called the activity's *float*. Float is a very

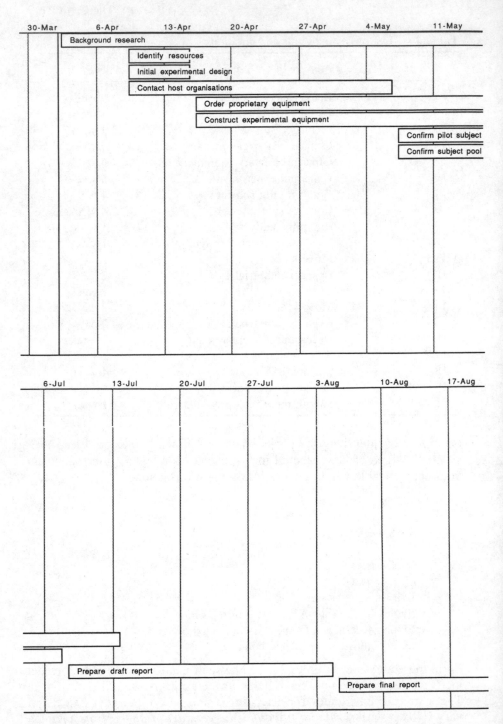

Figure 6.1 Gantt chart showing outline activities

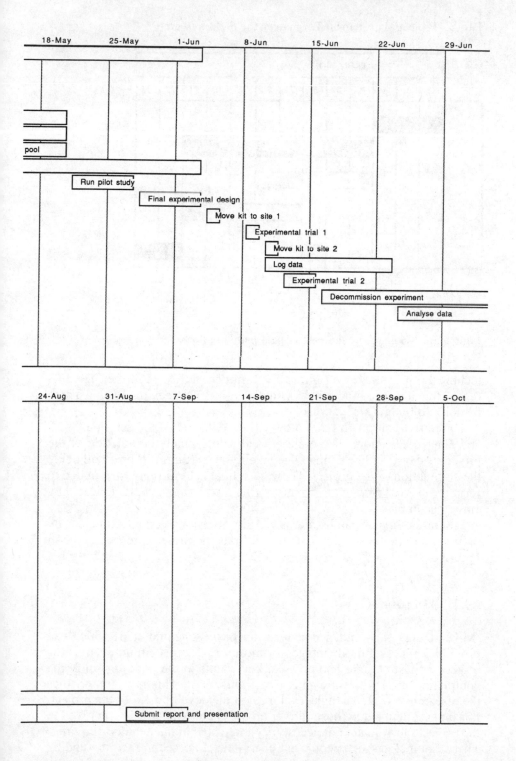

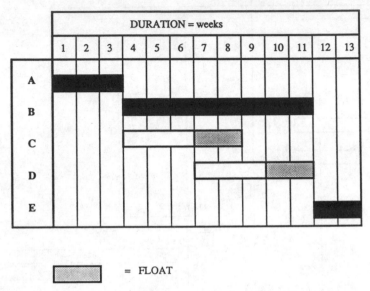

= FLOAT

Figure 6.2   Gantt chart showing critical path and float.

technical topic in its own right and will not be discussed further. Do note that in this instance if activity C is delayed by one week then D must also be delayed by one week.

To return to our main point, you will note that of all the activities, A, B and E have zero float. These are critical to the timely completion of the project because, unlike C and D, any delay in starting A, B or E will delay the completion of the project. These zero float activities are then linked to form the *critical path* of the project. Critical paths are usually indicated by emboldened bars.

Progress of a plan can be monitored simply enough on a Gantt chart by drawing outline bars which are shaded in as the project progresses, as in Figure 6.3.

28.2   Milestones

'Milestoning' is an enhancement to the basic schedule chart which can provide some useful advantages to monitoring and communicating the project. Milestones are laid down at key points in the plan to signify the completion of significant events (see Figure 6.2). This not only enables the researcher to keep a high-level grip on the development of the project, it is an excellent aid to those further up the chain who are also involved in the project but who are not necessarily interested in the detailed activities. These can include such people as supervisors, tutors, contractors, funding bodies, and so on. Milestones flag important events on the route to project completion. They should be few in number and the events should be natural.

Summary of section 28

1 The Gantt chart is a simple but effective method for scheduling projects against time.
2 To prepare a Gantt chart:
   (i)   Identify the key activities in your project.
   (ii) List them in order of dependence.
   (iii) Identify those activities which are critical to the viability of the project and link these into an activity chain: the critical path.
   (iv) Re-appraise resources.
3 Monitor progress of the plan by shading in the bars.
4 Use milestones to identify key points in the plan and to signify the completion of significant events.

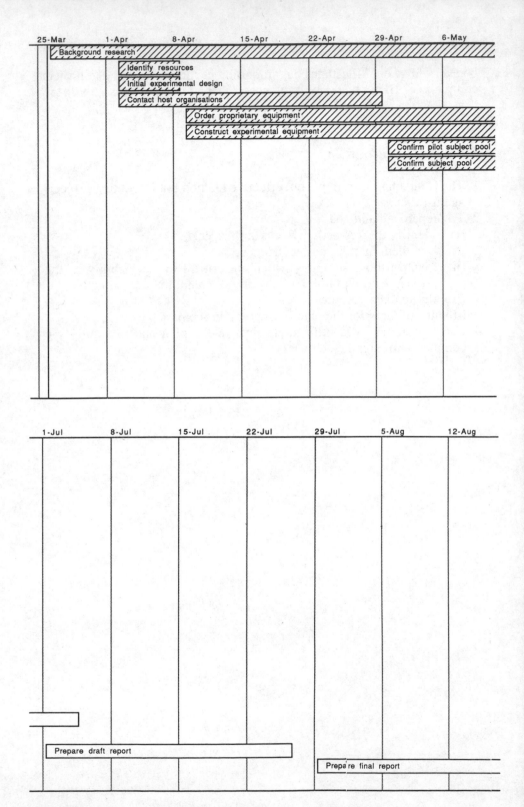

Figure 6.3 Progress chart with milestones.

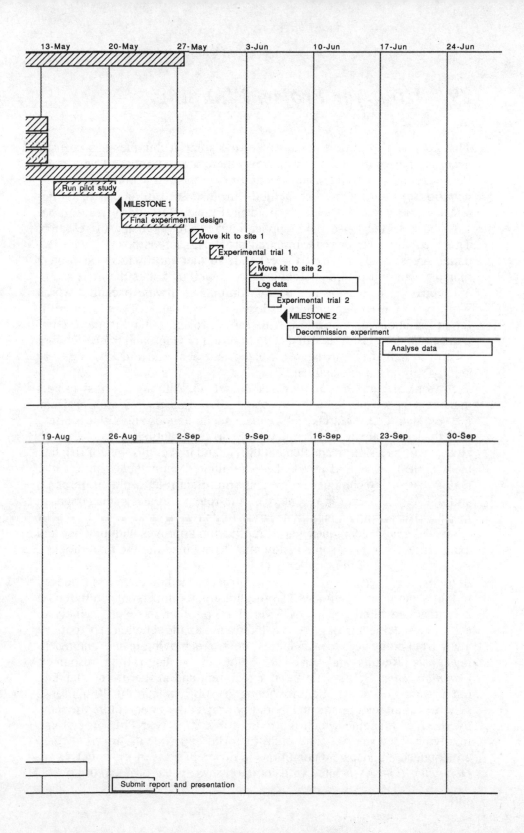

29   Hints for Project Planning

This approach to project management tools and techniques has been by necessity very superficial. Fortunately, there are a number of very good books around on project management for beginners in which Gantt charts, network schedules and other methods are discussed in much greater detail, and the interested reader should find these particularly fruitful, not least because they also have applications to areas outside of research. Those pursuing larger scale research projects, such as postgraduate students, are strongly advised to seek out further information on project management and planning techniques. As well as books there are available today an increasing number of computer software packages which will assist in analysing projects. Most will be capable of comparing different variations of schedule for the same project. Although these computer packages exist, it is still a key attraction of Gantt and many network schedules that they can be constructed and analysed quickly and very simply with just a pen and paper.

A word of caution is required at this stage. Although formal project management techniques are here being advocated for research projects, the very nature of research itself renders such methods slightly less effective than they are to say, engineering or construction tasks. Research always carries a significant element of risk and it is in this area of risk that basic project management tools become blunted. Nonetheless, it is undeniable that such techniques do have an important role to play in research and development, and in recent years the role of project management in research has become a legitimate study in its own right.

As with many techniques whose application improves with practice and experience, there exist some handy hints to engineering the final product. Below are a few of the simpler ones.

Activities and goals. In discussing the project schedule there is a tendency to talk about doing 'activities'. Unfortunately, too much concentration on activities can blind one to the overall purpose of the plan; namely to achieve a specific aim or goal. When drawing up the schedule, try to move away from doing activities and think more of achieving results and reaching goals. Results and goals are achieved by controlling resources.

Common sense. Be realistic in your planning and in the use of planning tools. A memory experiment involving 20 subjects learning 40 nonsense syllables as an undergraduate laboratory project does not require the same overhead in planning which is needed for a three-year PhD programme involving, for example, nine multi-factorial experiments, four of which are conducted under field conditions in different parts of the country.

Decomposition. Associated with common sense is the problem of how far should tasks be broken down into their activities. That is, at what level of decomposition of the project should the experimenter call a halt? Clearly there is a trap of *reductio ad absurdum* and it is possible to go too far. There are no hard and fast rules here and knowing when to stop the breakdown of activities into further activities is an experience which is soon learned. Any breakdown will depend on the complexity of the overall plan and on the type of activity being carried out. There is, of course, no reason why you cannot have different levels of plans, with each lower level possessing a greater degree of complexity than the one above. The top level plans would be ideal for briefing purposes and monitoring progress. This would, of course, only apply to the larger scale projects.

Startlines. When determining activities, use start time rather than finish time. Herein lies a problem which is commonly reflected in the tendency which people have to focus their attention on deadlines rather than startlines. They gauge their work by how late they can leave it rather than how early they can start it. Concentration on start times will produce 'unexpected' free time. This time can be used either to contain those problems which may occur en route or can be freely offered up to other projects or activities.

Expected time. Some planners allow three time estimates for each event, the earliest time (optimistic time), the latest time (pessimistic time), and the expected time (most likely time). The use of expected time ensures that the plan is realistic, both in its application, and in the calculation and utilisation of free time.

Plan early. Plan to start all activities as early as possible and connect them to the schedule as late as possible.

Parallelism. You will often find that certain activities can be organized to run in parallel. These parallel activities should be maximized.

Activity accuracy. The shorter the duration of an activity the more accurate it is.

Start at the end. When drawing up the plan enter the finish date first of all (e.g. the submission date for the dissertation) then work backwards identifying all those activities which need to be completed before the end point can be reached.

Summary of section 29

1 Any plan is designed to simulate a project as it will exist in real life. Every project is unique and to maximize the chances of a successful outcome it must be planned in detail.
2 For a project to be planned it must be decomposable. That is, it must be capable of:
   (a) being broken down into discreet elements (activities, tasks, jobs);

(b) running each element either in sequence or in parallel;

(c) estimating and assigning a duration to each element;

(d) establishing start and finish times for each element.

3 Various techniques exist for the formal planning of projects (e.g. Gantt charts and network schedules) but their underlying principles are similar. These follow the sequence:

(i)   Identify all activities.

(ii)   List these activities in order of dependence.

(iii) Assign each activity a start time, end time and duration.

(iv) Identify the critical path.

4 Formal scheduling of a project has the following advantages:

(a) it forces the planner to think out the project in detail.

(b) it enables resources (including time) to be scheduled.

(c) it allows the planner to try out and compare different plans for the same project with relative ease.

(d) it encourages commitment from others to a well thought out and achievable goal.

(e) once under way it will allow progress to be monitored.

5 The nature of research is such that all plans will carry a degree of experimental risk. This risk must be addressed in any project plan.

6 Do not forget that at some point your project must meet the real world. When it does it will be tested under fire. If your plan has been meticulously and sensibly constructed your project will stand firm.

SAQ 18
Why bother with formal planning? How can it help your research project?

SAQ 19
The planning is complete. Now what must you do?

Appendix 1 Ethical Principles for Conducting Research with Human Participants

The following 'Revised Ethical Principles' is reproduced from *The Psychologist,* **13**(6) June 1990, pp. 269–72, by kind permission of The British Psychological Society.

1 Introduction

1.1 The principles given below are intended to apply to research with human participants. Principles of conduct in professional practice are to be found in the Society's Code of Conduct and in the advisory documents prepared by the Divisions, Sections and Special Groups of the Society.

1.2 Participants in psychological research should have confidence in the investigators. Good psychological research is possible only if there is mutual respect and confidence between investigators and participants. Psychological investigators are potentially interested in all aspects of human behaviour and conscious experience. However, for ethical reasons, some areas of human experiences and behaviour may be beyond the reach of experiment, observation or other form of psychological investigation. Ethical guidelines are necessary to clarify the conditions under which psychological research is acceptable.

1.3 The principles given below supplement for researchers with human participants the general ethical principles of members of the Society as stated in the British Psychological Society's Code of Conduct (1985). Members of the British Psychological Society are expected to abide by both the Code of Conduct and the fuller principles expressed here. Members should also draw the principles to the attention of research colleagues who are not members of the Society. Members should encourage colleagues to adopt them and ensure that they are followed by all researchers whom they supervise (e.g. research assistants, postgraduate, undergraduate, A-Level and GCSE students).

1.4 In recent years, there has been an increase in legal actions by members of the general public against professionals for alleged misconduct. Researchers must recognise the possibility of such legal action if they infringe the rights and dignity of participants in their research.

2   General

2.1 In all circumstances, investigators must consider the ethical implications and psychologial consequences for the participants in their research. The essential principle is that the investigation should be considered from the standpoint of all participants; foreseeable threats to their psychological well-being, health, values or dignity should be eliminated. Investigators should recognise that, in our multi-cultural and multi-ethnic society and where investigations involve individuals of different ages, gender and social background, the investigators may not have sufficient knowledge of the implications of an investigation for the participants. It should be borne in mind that the best judges of whether an investigation will cause offence may be members of the population from which the participants in the research are to be drawn.

3   Consent

3.1 Whenever possible, the investigator should inform all participants of the objectives of the investigation. The investigator should inform the participants of all aspects of the research or intervention that might reasonably be expected to influence willingness to participate. The investigator should, normally, explain all other aspects of the research or intervention about which the participants enquire. Failure to make full disclosure prior to obtaining informed consent requires additional safeguards to protect the welfare and dignity of the participants (see Section 4).
3.2 Research with children or with participants who have impairments that will limit understanding and/or communication such that they are unable to give their real consent requires special safeguarding procedures.
3.3 Where possible, the real consent of children and of adults with impairments in understanding or communication should be obtained. In addition, where research involves all persons under sixteen years of age, consent should be obtained from parents or from those *in loco parentis*.
3.4 Where real consent cannot be obtained from adults with impairments in understanding or communication, wherever possible the investigator should consult a person well-placed to appreciate the participant's reaction, such as a member of the person's family, and must obtain the disinterested approval of the research from independent advisors.
3.5 When research is being conducted with detained persons, particular care should be taken over informed consent, paying attention to the

special circumstances which may affect the person's ability to give free informed consent.

3.6 Investigators should realise that they are often in a position of authority or influence over participants who may be their students, employees or clients. This relationship must not be allowed to pressurise the participants to take part in, or remain in, an investigation.

3.7 The payment of participants must not be used to induce them to risk harm beyond that which they risk without payment in their normal lifestyle.

3.8 If harm, unusual discomfort, or other negative consequences for the individual's future life might occur, the investigator must obtain the disinterested approval of independent advisors, inform the participants, and obtain informed, real consent from each of them.

3.9 In longitudinal research, consent may need to be obtained on more than one occasion.

4 Deception

4.1 The withholding of information or the misleading of participants is unacceptable if the participants are typically likely to object or show unease once debriefed. Where this is in any doubt, appropriate consultation must precede the investigation. Consultation is best carried out with individuals who share the social and cultural background of the participants in the research, but the advice of ethics committees or experienced and disinterested colleagues may be sufficient.

4.2 Intentional deception of the participants over the purpose and general nature of the investigation should be avoided whenever possible. Participants should never be deliberately misled without extremely strong scientific or medical justification. Even then there should be strict controls and the disinterested approval of independent advisors.

4.3 It may be impossible to study some psychological processes without withholding information about the true object of the study or deliberately misleading the participants. Before conducting such a study, the investigator has a special responsibility to (a) determine that alternative procedures avoiding concealment or deception are not available; (b) ensure that the participants are provided with sufficient information at the earliest stage; and (c) consult appropriately upon the way that the withholding of information or deliberate deception will be received.

5 Debriefing

5.1 In studies where the participants are aware that they have taken part in an investigation, when the data have been collected, the investigator should provide the participants with any necessary information to complete their understanding of the nature of the research. The investigator should discuss with the participants their experience of the research in order to monitor any unforeseen negative effects or misconceptions.

5.2 Debriefing does not provide a justification for unethical aspects of an investigation.

5.3 Some effects which may be produced by an experiment will not be negated by a verbal description following the research. Investigators have a responsibility to ensure that participants receive any necessary debriefing in the form of active intervention before they leave the research setting.

6 Withdrawal from the Investigation

6.1 At the onset of the investigation investigators should make plain to participants their right to withdraw from the research at any time, irrespective of whether or not payment or other inducement has been offered. It is recognised that this may be difficult in certain observational or organisational settings, but nevertheless the investigator must attempt to ensure that participants (including children) know of their right to withdraw. When testing children, avoidance of the testing situation may be taken as evidence of failure to consent to the procedure and should be acknowledged.

6.2 In the light of experience of the investigation, or as a result of debriefing, the participant has the right to withdraw retrospectively any consent given, and to require that their own data, including recordings, be destroyed.

7 Confidentiality

7.1 Subject to the requirement of legislation, including the Data Protection Act, information obtained about a participant during an investigation is confidential unless otherwise agreed in advance. Investigators who are put under pressure to disclose condifential information should draw this point to the attention of those exerting such pressure. Participants in psychological research have a right to expect that information they provide will be treated confidentially and, if published, will not be identifiable as theirs. In the event that confidentiality and/or anonymity cannot be guaranteed, the participant must be warned of this in advance of agreeing to participate.

8   Protection of participants

8.1 Investigators have a primary responsibility to protect participants from physical and mental harm during the investigation. Normally, the risk of harm must be no greater than in ordinary life, i.e. participants should not be exposed to risks greater than or additional to those encountered in their normal lifestyles. Where the risk of harm is greater than in ordinary life the provisions of 3.8 should apply. Participants must be asked about any factors in the procedure that might create a risk, such as pre-existing medical conditions, and must be advised of any special action they should take to avoid risk.
8.2 Participants should be informed of procedures for contacting the investigator within a reasonable time period following participation should stress, potential harm, or related questions or concern arise despite the precautions required by these Principles. Where research procedures might result in undesirable consequences for participants, the investigator has the responsibility to detect and remove or correct these consequences.
8.3 Where research may involve behaviour or experiences that participants may regard as personal and private the participants must be protected from stress by all appropriate measures, including the assurance that answers to personal questions need not be given. There should be no concealment or deception when seeking information that might encroach on privacy.
8.4 In research involving children, great caution should be exercised when discussing the results with parents, teachers or others *in loco parentis*, since evaluative statements may carry unintended weight.

9   Observational research

9.1 Studies based upon observation must respect the privacy and psychological well-being of the individuals studied. Unless those observed give their consent to being observed, observational research is only acceptable in the situations where those observed would expect to be observed by strangers. Additionally, particular account should be taken of local cultural values and of the possibility of intruding upon the privacy of individuals who, even while in a normally public space, may believe they are unobserved.

10   Giving advice

10.1 During research, an investigator may obtain evidence of psychological or physical problems of which a participant is, apparently, unaware. In

147

such a case, the investigator has a responsibility to inform the participant if the investigator believes that by not doing so the participant's future well-being may be endangered.

10.2 If, in the normal course of psychological research, or as a result of problems detected as in 10.1, a participant solicits advice concerning educational, personality, behavioural or health issues, caution should be exercised. If the issue is serious and the investigator is not qualified to offer assistance, the appropriate source of professional advice should be recommended. Further details of the giving of advice will be found in the Society's Code of Conduct.

10.3 In some kinds of investigation the giving of advice is appropriate if this forms an intrinsic part of the research and has been agreed in advance.

11 Colleagues

11.1 Investigators share responsibility for the ethical treatment of research participants with their collaborators, assistants, students and employees. A psychologist who believes that another psychologist or investigator may be conducting research that is not in accordance with the principles above should encourage that investigator to re-evaluate the research.

Answers to SAQs

SAQ 1
The danger here is that applied psychology can finish up consisting of little more than a collection of data which, although correct in itself, has no worth beyond the specific problem which each addressed. The data possess little or no predictive value. Prediction is a requirement for psychological theory. The applied experimentalist will seek to relate his or her findings to general psychological theory.

SAQ 2
(a) The independent variable is the gas supply, either air or oxygen.
(b) The dependent variable is the ability to make correct decisions.
(c) The hypothesis predicts that firemen will make more correct decisions when breathing pure oxygen than when breathing air.

SAQ 3
This study is quite high on internal validity. The experimental design is strong so one can assume that extraneous variance is controlled and, therefore, one is confident that any significant differences in performance on the maze task are due to differences in illumination.
   On the other hand this study is low in external validity. Remember that the question concerned the welding performance of experienced professional welders under different levels of illumination, and in particular that increasing light intensity would decrease welding speed over what is quite a long fillet of weld (12 metres). Given this, the sample of students is not a good representation of the population of welders. Consequently, any transfer or generalizing of results will be weak.

SAQ 4
In practice it means that the applied psychologist must be prepared to put him or herself out to understand the work practices of the host organization and any constraints which will impinge on the experimental design. Such constraints usually exist for operational and/or safety reasons.

SAQ 5
Simply by observation of the natural world.

SAQ 6
(a) The key positive indicator in an aim is the preposition 'To . . .'.
(b) The key negative indicator is the conjunction '. . . and . . .'. If 'and' appears anywhere in your aim then you have not made it precise enough.

SAQ 7

Although a purely random sample is theoretically possible, it is not a practical situation. With limited resources you are likely to exclude, for example, all Catholic priests or Methodist ministers while including representations from other groups such as Baptists or the Church of Scotland. In this instance it would be appropriate to use a stratified sample where each Christian sect is represented. Individual members of each sect, or strata, can then be selected by random methods.

SAQ 8

(a) The problem is simply that at the outset the selection would not be random. The decision to select every 50th person is predetermined and, therefore, no-one else on the list has a chance of being selected.

(b) You advise that every 50th person can be selected providing the first person is chosen randomly. Your random number generator might give you the number 37, in which case you ask the insurance company to enter their list at the person who is number 87 (37 + 50) followed thereafter by every 50th person on the list: 137, 187 . . . etc.

SAQ 9

The most common cause is a lack of appreciation of *time*.

SAQ 10

It forces the researcher to bring an essential discipline to bear on his or her project, and to do so at a very early stage of the programme.

SAQ 11

At the very least, one. Thereafter as many as are required to ensure that you are comfortable in your own mind that the main experiment will run according to plan. In most cases much can be learned from just one pilot. If a major problem is highlighted then this part may frequently be re-tested without the need to run the whole pilot.

SAQ 12

When you are physically or operationally debarred from one or more of your treatment conditions. You must be sure that the data obtained from a primed experiment are sound. That is, they are not likely to be corrupted during their collection by a third party.

SAQ 13

Because each serves a different function. The experimental diary is an operational log concerned with the collection and processing of research data. The site diary is the administrative log for the project. Keeping the diaries separate avoids confusing these two functions.

150

SAQ 14
Because it is too public. Group pressure can force many people to 'volunteer' for things against their own wishes.

SAQ 15
Good office organization reduces workloads and administrative procedures, and produces a clear working atmosphere. This is important even if you are working by yourself.

SAQ 16
Ensure that
(a) your 'office' is well organized;
(b) your procedures for data collection and processing are simple;
(c) your record keeping is efficient, and
(d) your records are secure.

SAQ 17
By establishing a clear aim for your project and drawing up a functional specification for the research programme.

SAQ 18
Formal planning provides you and others involved in your research with a top-level description of the overall project. Planning provides you with the ability to better
(a) evaluate different ideas;
(b) raise commitment amongst others;
(c) provide realistic start and finish dates, and
(d) identify those critical factors which underpin the success or failure of the whole project.

SAQ 19
You and your plan must meet the real world. *Thinking* has to be followed by *doing*.

Bibliography

ANON (1966) Experience with *Gemini* solves EVA problems. *Aerospace Medicine*, **37**, 1284–6.

BARTLETT, F.C. (1951) *The Mind at Work and Play*. London: Allen & Unwin.

BELBIN, E. (1979) Applicable psychology and some national problems. *Bulletin of the British Psychological Society*, **32**, 241–4.

BLUM, M.L. and NAYLOR, J.C. (1968) *Industrial Psychology: Its Theoretical and Social Foundations*. London: Harper & Row.

BRANDT, R.M. (1972) *Studying Behaviour in Natural Settings*, Eastbourne: Holt, Rinehart & Winston, Inc.

BRITISH PSYCHOLOGICAL SOCIETY, THE (1978) Ethical principles for research with human subjects. *Bulletin of the British Psychological Society*, **31**, 48–9.

BRITISH PSYCHOLOGICAL SOCIETY, THE (1985) A code of conduct for psychologists. *Bulletin of the British Psychological Society*, **38**, 41–3.

BROADBENT, D.E. (1971) Relation between theory and application in psychology. In P.B. Warr (ed.), *Psychology at Work*, pp. 15–30. Harmondsworth: Penguin Books.

BROOKS, F.P. (1982) *The Mythical Man-Month*. Mass: Addison-Wesley.

CANTER, D. (1985) *Applying Psychology*. Inaugural lecture, May 1985. University of Surrey.

CHAPANIS, A. (1967) The relevance of laboratory studies to practical situations. *Ergonomics*, **10**(5) 557–77.

CHRISTOPHERSON, D., BOYD, R., FLEMING, I., MACDONALD, I., MYLROI, M., WARDLOW, A. and WILLMOTT, J. (1983) *Research Student and Supervisor: an approach to good supervisory practice*. Polaris House, Swindon: SERC.

ELLIOTT, E. (1960) Perception and alertness. *Ergonomics*, **3**, 357–64.

GODDEN, D.R. (1975). Cold, wet and hostile. *New Behaviour*, June, pp. 422–5.

GREENE, J. and D'OLIVEIRA, M. (1990) *Learning to Use Statistical Tests in Psychology*. Milton Keynes: Open University Press.

HAMMERTON, M. (1967) Simulators for training. *Electronics and Power*, **13**, 8–10.

HARRIS, P. (1986) *Designing and Reporting Experiments*. Milton Keynes: Open University Press.

HILGARD, E.R. (1964) A perspective on the relationship between learning theory and educational practices. In *Theories of Learning and Instruction 63rd Yearbook*. Chicago: National Society for the Study of Education.

LEVI-STRAUSS, C. (1977) *Structural Anthropology*. London: Allen Lane.

MASTERS, W.J. and JOHNSON, V.E. (1966) *Human Sexual Response*. Boston: Little, Brown & Co.

SILVERMANN, I. (1977) *The Human Subject in the Psychology Laboratory*. New York: Pergamon Press.

TAYLOR, F.V. (1960) Four basic ideas in engineering psychology. In D.H. Holding (ed.), *Experimental Psychology in Industry*. Harmondsworth: Penguin Books.

WARR, P.B. (1971) *Psychology at Work*. Harmondsworth: Penguin.

WASON, P.C. and JOHNSON-LAIRD, P.N. (1968) *Thinking and Reasoning*. Harmondsworth: Penguin.

WATERS, S.J. (1988) *'3Cs' of Successful IT Projects*. Bristol Polytechnic: Department of Mathematics and Computer Science.

ZWAGA. H. (1988). Buying a ticket for the Washington Metro. In D. Megow (ed.), *Contemporary Ergonomics*. London: Taylor & Francis.

Index